REPARATIONS!
&
GOD'S JUDGMENT

John D. Brinson

Resource *Publications*

An imprint of *Wipf and Stock Publishers*
199 West 8th Avenue • Eugene OR 97401

Resource Publications
An imprint of *Wipf and Stock Publishers*
199 West 8th Avenue, Suite 3
Eugene, Oregon 97401

Reparations & God's Judgment
By Brinson, John D.
Copyright©2002 Brinson, John D.
ISBN: 1-57910-988-8
Publication Date: June, 2002

PREFACE

This book seeks to present evidence that illustrates for African Americans (my people) that we are legally and morally due compensation for the theft of our ancestors' labor, our labor currently, and the mental and physical brokenness we still suffer as a legacy of slavery. This is the sole purpose for this book. Its intent is not to stroke scholars and convince them about how scholarly I am, or could be, but rather to pull your coat to what you have lost and how you can get it back. If this book opens the eyes of one person I shall consider it successful.

I shall present eyewitness accounts of the horrors we have and still are suffering at the hands of our oppressors. Some evidence from eyewitness accounts, scholars, newspapers, and other documents that report on the role the U.S. government, state governments, Armed Forces, Police Departments, KKK (and other terrorist groups) and many individuals have played in the oppression of our ancestors.

I have also drawn on Old and New Testament texts, including Jesus Christ, in an effort to show you that reparation is due us and that God (Yahweh) wants us to have it. I believe the more information we have on a situation, the easier it is for us to make the correct decisions concerning how we should resolve it. In the near future, America is going to be served a past due bill and most white Americans, will refuse and resist any efforts exerted to collect. However, on the other hand, history indicates some white people will support us. The temptation to acquiesce to the oppressors' desire will overwhelm some of us and cause us to become filled with fear and apathy. History however, indicates that when our people

(African Americans) have the facts and believe they are right, they will struggle until victory. It is my personal belief that the struggle for reparations will prove to be the paramount and final passionate struggle for Africans throughout the world.

I dedicate this book to all the brothers and sisters who are, or have been involved in the Reparations Movement, and by all means to those of you who shall become part of the Movement.

Thanks to Dr. Michael S. Williams for his encouragement in this project.

I thank God (Yahweh) for blessing me and calling me to his ministry and providing me with the determination to complete this book.

John D. Brinson

CONTENTS

Preface   i

Forward   v

Introduction   ix

SECTION I.   The Charges and Evidence   1

SECTION II.   Marks of Oppression   53

SECTION III.   The Indicted Criminals   59

SECTION IV.   Modern Examples of Reparations   85

SECTION V.   Reparations & the Judean/Christian Context   115

Appendix.   149

Bibliography.   157

FOREWORD

Reparations! And Gods Judgment, is a difficult book to read. I say that it is difficult to read, not because of its complexity, but because of the discomfort it can cause. It can cause a great deal of discomfort to the beneficiaries of the sweat and toil of Africans brought to these shores nearly four centuries ago. It can even cause some difficulty to the descendants of those Africans now existing in America. Why? Because to the first group, it would be easy to say, "I didn't enslave anyone! My grandfather came over to this country with nothing, he worked for everything he got!" "Why don't *you people* quit complaining and learn the value of hard work." "If my ancestors could flee Czarist Russia, Hapsburg Austria, or Nazi Germany, land at New York's Ellis Island and then pull themselves up by their boot straps, why can't *your* people do the same?" To this first group, I would say, had it not been for the brutal economic exploitation of Africans forcibly dragged to the so-called New World, then, your grandfather would not have had a place to flee to! And also remember, had not Western Europeans forcibly appropriated the Western Hemisphere from the Red Man, then there would have been *no* Ellis Island to land on! Regardless as to how we may want to look at it, there can be *no* wealth without poverty. There can be no privilege without discrimination.

To the second group, Africans in America, I would address your discomfort at this document by answering your question before you ask it. Your question would perhaps be "why bring all of this up?" You would probably also ask, "can't we let bygones be bygones?" Of course we could, if we lived on another planet! We are Africans existing in America - on planet Earth! The question of whether we arrived on slave ships from Africa or crowded steamers in steerage on ships from Europe around the turn of this century was settled nearly four centuries ago. In 1619, a Dutch warship encountered a Spanish slave ship, took the cargo, twenty Africans, and dropped them off at Jamestown, Virginia - then Great Britain's first colony in North America. For nearly forty years, these Africans, those that descended from them, and those that followed, were considered "indentured servants" That, meant they were to be granted freedom after a certain number of years. During that period, they were to literally work for *free* or very little. By 1660, the situation changed. Africans as a cheap source of labor became so valuable that what had started out as an arrangement to work for several years, degenerated to *slavery for life* based on the *color of their skin*! America would never have become the great industrial power that it is today, had it not been for the Africans, and their descendants, which originally landed at Jamestown, Virginia in 1619.

The rights and privileges granted to all American citizens were denied to Africans by the successor to the British political establishment, the United States of America, after its successful rebellion against the British Crown, which began in earnest in 1776. Just as the African toiled for the British, he toiled for the American. His free labor created the economic environment for the fortunes many of our so-called "Founding Fathers" and maintained the comfortable lifestyles of such members of the landed gentry as George Washington and Thomas Jefferson.

This system of labor was very similar to the riches and comfort acquired by the Nazis as they enslaved and butchered those they deemed to be "sub-human," i.e., Jews, Eastern Europeans, and other slave laborers forcibly removed from their occupied countries in Western Europe during World War II! Without this slave labor, the genocidal Nazi machine would never have been able to burn, loot, and pillage Europe. Without our forebear's slave labor, the Europeans, like the Nazis that followed them, would not have been able to burn, loot, and pillage this great land. And as our friends in the worldwide Jewish community are now demanding-and rightfully so—an accounting of their wealth sitting in banks around the world where the Nazis had deposited it over a half-century ago, so must we!

I thank God for the toil and long hours of faithful research that Reverend Brinson put into this volume. No thoughtful person of African descent existing in America can justify not reading this book and taking its message to heart!

Rev. Michael S. Williams, D.Min.
Bayview Hunters Point
San Francisco, California,

INTRODUCTION

In 1441 two Portuguese explorer ships met off the West Coast of Africa and decided to attack the people on the coast. Under the cover of the darkness of night, while the people were asleep in their encampment, they attacked and killed four men and carried off ten captives. Shortly thereafter, the Portuguese outfitted six ships for war and attacked the Africans. A "small-scale war" took place on the West Coast of Africa and one hundred and sixty-five men, women, and children were taken captive. This was the battle that started the ball rolling to the battles we are currently engaged in that are part of a larger war.

The war continues and can be traced historically through our resistance to the initial attacks against us in 1441; the mutinies on many slave ships; insurrections on the plantations and in the revolts of the ghettoes since slavery. It can be seen in the deadly physical violence unleashed regularly on Africans and African Americans in particular, by white citizens, as well as, members of their police departments. It can be seen in the lack of job opportunities and the economic inequalities that racism breeds, nurtures and spreads thoroughly and relentlessly throughout the political and economic systems. When we are fortunate enough to be gainfully employed, it can be seen in the theft of our labor. The practice of paying an African American considerably less than a white for doing the same job and expending the same amount of labor constitutes theft of labor. It can be seen in the segregation of housing. Most African Americans dwell in the police-controlled Bantustans (ghettoes) in many of the large cities. It can be seen in the fact that whenever we try to exercise the rights of the citizenry, special Acts must be passed. Citizens and non-black others never need special meetings of Congress and new laws to exercise the rights of citizenry.

The continuation of the war can be noted in the attitudes of many of our oppressors. This war against Africans and African Americans, in particular, is evidenced in the political, social, and economic institutions as well as in the minds and hearts of the citizens of the United States of America.

Besides the unjust war being perpetrated against us, and the stealing of our labor, there is a mountain of psychological damage we still suffer as a legacy of chattel slavery. We have been, and are physically and psychologically oppressed to the edge of destruction. We witness our children walking along its edges daily as many are pushed, or pulled over that edge and fall into chaos. We are no longer whole persons, but rather broken pieces meandering down the highway of life without any idea of where we are headed. Someone, or something has cracked our skulls open and drained our knowledge of ourselves from our minds and refilled it with something we cannot become. A part of our brokenness is a result of the promise of what we could become and the reality of humans and their institutions obstructing and preventing it.

God, as depicted in the Judeo/Christian tradition, supports reparations for us. Reparation is the return of stolen goods in Biblical tradition, thereby making things the way they were. This is evidenced in God's plan for the Hebrews in His liberation of them from Egypt.

It is our God given right to seek the return of our inheritance (stolen labor of our ancestors) and our right minds. If this situation is not made right and just, and because God is just, His judgment is upon the oppressive thief and perhaps the "fire next time" will soon be upon us.

John. D. Brinson, M/Div.

SECTION 1

THE CHARGES
AND THE EVIDENCE

THE CHARGES

While motivated by profits, Europeans and others waged an unjust war against our ancestors. They kidnapped millions of them, stole their labor, caused pain and death to countless numbers, and provided a treatment so cruel that it traumatized millions bringing mental sickness in them. This sickness has been passed down through the generations and become actualized by the forces of the dynamics of neo-slavery. This continuing oppressive situation provides the environment that maintains the negative behavior in our community and the perpetual conflict between our African Nation and the White Nation.

The evidence presented is drawn from personal accounts of eyewitnesses, letters, legal documents, historians, sociologists, psychologists, and others. I have tried to keep my personal opinion subdued, but it surfaces occasionally. However, the evidence speaks for itself.

This evidence is presented to you in an effort shed some light on the war we are in, the theft of our ancestors' labor, the psychological trauma they suffered, and the effects this whole dynamic has on our generation. We find ourselves today reacting to racism, segregation, and economic discrimination with the same negative actions and reactions as our ancestors under the chattel slave system. We are a physically broken and psychologically shattered people and white Americans,

Europeans, and their governments are the responsible villains. You are the judge and jury of this case. It happened to your ancestors, and you are its victim today. Do not surrender your right to require and expect justice at all times, in all situations.

Reader, your duty is to read the evidence, and bring back a just and legal verdict.

EVIDENCE

Chapter 1

THE UNJUST WAR
AGAINST AFRICAN PEOPLES

Webster defines war as a determined attack, a condition of conflict, armed or otherwise. Utilizing this definition I am prepared to claim Europeans, Americans, Christian churches, and Jewish synagogues have been engaged in a racist war (determined attack) against our people for many centuries. We live most of our daily lives defensively, struggling to survive in the quagmire of this continuing racial conflict.

War can also be defined as the process of politics taken to its military conclusion. As Huey P. Newton[1] claimed, "war is politics with a gun" or, Mao Tse Tung[2] "politics grows from the barrel of a gun." An act of war is politics taken to its military conclusion by one nation against another or between groups in a nation. Is the violence used by the protectors of the system, such as Police Departments, National Guard, the Army and other organized white groups, to control African Americans, acts of war? Were the attacks on the West Coast of Africa, the kidnapping of our ancestors, their forced transit across the oceans, and the taking of their labor, acts of war?

Imari Abubakari Obadele, the president of the provisional government of the African American, defines our relationship

---
[1] Co-Founder with Bobby Seale of the Black Panther Party.
[2] Chairman of China.

with the United States government and its people as a state of war.

> The landless new African nation in America during time of slavery arose from the forced mingling of persons from several African sub-races, admixed with some Amerindian and European racial strains, and bound by a distinct common history and culture. This new African nation was subjected to a warfare by the United States as brutal as any ever waged by one people against another. New African manpower was destroyed during slavery under the white American nearly as systematically as Jewish manpower under the Nazis, with the major exceptions being (1) a high rate of replacement of destroyed Africans by births and new imports, and (2) a design in America, after 1800, to minimize physical destruction while ruthlessly pursuing cultural destruction.[3]

By definition our situation and our consistent struggles against it, indicates we are in a state of war (conflict, often armed) with Europeans and the United States' government and its citizens.

Politics is war through words and laws in deciding who gets what and how much. When politics become ineffective in acquiring the planned goal, the oppressor escalates his assault until his objectives are realized. Paul Boutelle admits the following utility of politics in the control of African Americans:

> The policies that determine how they will live are made by others and imposed on them. Every aspect of African American life is governed by

---

[3] Imari Abubakari Obadele. *Foundations of the Black Nation*. Detroit: 1975. p.82.

the Democratic and Republican agents of the capitalist rulers of this country. Their actions (or in-actions) perpetuate in-equality, poverty, degradation, police brutality, insecurity, unemployment, low-paying jobs, bad schools, inadequate housing, and medical facilities, a shorter life span and all the other evils suffered by black Americans.[4]

The current struggles and battles of the war we are engaged in for our survival are not rooted in the present, but has an origin that extends back to ancient times when the veil of history just begins to lift and let light in. This is the period around the end of the last great Ice Age according to many scholars. This is the period when the great Cushite (black) civilization flourished. Many antiquarians claim this great civilization extended around the equator of the world, emanating from Africa and spreading northwards and eastwards, bringing knowledge and civilization to the world. This was a matriarchal civilization, meaning women ruled and were held in high esteem. Lineage passed through them and they were revered. They were the objects of adoration and worship as attested by the many statuettes of them discovered throughout the world. Europeans were living in caves during this period and were patriarchal in their world-view. European women were held in low esteem because they were considered a liability during the period of pastoral wanderings. Inheritance flowed through the eldest son.

The ancient Cushite matriarchal-based civilization was destroyed or conquered by the so-called Aryans. They swept down from the mountains and steppes, which had been their habitat for centuries as they struggled to survive in the cold, sunless environment of ice and snow. Now, they were on the

---

[4] Paul Boutelle The Case for a Black Party (N.Y 1968) p.6.

march to world domination utilizing a "scorched earth" policy and the harshness of the environment they had survived more than adequately provided them with the will and ferociousness to destroy, conquer, and take what they wanted.

Somewhere around 4000 BC, according to noted scholar, Dr Chancellor Williams[5], they reached the frontiers of Egypt and began to attack her. They became successful somewhere around the second millennia before the present era. Under the tribal name Hyksos these invaders from the north conquered Egypt and held political control for several centuries. Following brief respites, they re-conquered and ruled Egypt intermittently as Persians, Greeks, Romans, Arabs, etc.

This rather recent phase of the war against us has its origin approximately 500 years ago, when subjects of Portugal during their exploratory wanderings over the world attacked the West Coast of Africa. They kidnapped several Africans and forcibly carried them back to Portugal as a gift for Prince Henry. Henry realized the potential for profits and secured an audience with the Pope. Prince Henry and the Pope made a deal in which Portugal would be affirmed in its engagement in warfare on the West Coast of Africa to secure captives, providing they were proselytized to Christianity. This was the beginning of the horrendous Atlantic slave trade. Our ancestors resisted the initial attack by the Portuguese, and a "small-scale war took place on the West Coast of Africa. Sixty-five Africans were captured in this battle."[6]

From the very first, our ancestors struggled against their oppressive situation (state of conflict) physically and mentally. When aboard those horrific slave ships, many of them resisted by starving themselves preferring death to captivity. Starvation was so common that a special instrument called a "speculum oris" (or mouth opener) was carried aboard these ships. It was used to force the resisting captive's mouth open so food could

---

[5] *Destruction of Black Civilizations*.
[6] Anne Terry White. *Human Cargoes* (Champaign, IL 1972) p.13.

be poured in through a funnel to prevent starvation. "Even the speculum oris sometimes failed with a slave determined to die."[7]

Others threw themselves overboard. Example: At Saint Christopher, April 1737, there was a mass suicide attempt on the ship, *Prince of Orange*.[8]

Many resisted by utilizing mutiny on the cargo ships. There were over 150 such violent battles. Mannix and Cowley claim the following in the book, *Black Cargoes*:

> There are fairly detailed accounts on approximately fifty-five mutinies on slavers from 1699 to 1845, not to mention passing references to more than a hundred others.[9]

The most well known mutinous revolt occurred on a ship named Amistad. A captive named Cinque led it. There was a movie recently playing in the theaters about this story. Stephen Spielberg produced this movie about a segment of our holocaust after our children illustrated to him in one of our Oakland, California schools, how irritated they were from hearing about the holocaust of other peoples (Jews) without other people hearing about our (African) holocaust. I suppose this pricked his conscience and motivated him out of a certain goodness, to try and show in someway that he understood and cared.

In America during chattel slavery countless conspiracies and open rebellions against the racist and oppressive forces in the lives of the slaves took place. One white scholar, Dr. Herbert Aptheker, claims there were hundreds of rebellions and conspiracies that took place between 1526 and 1864.[10]

---

[7] Daniel P. Mannix. *Black Cargoes* (N.Y. 1962) p.119.
[8] James Pope-Hennessy. *A Study of the Atlantic Slave Trade* (N.Y.1967) p.105.
[9] Ibid., p.111
[10] Herbert Aptheker. *Negro Slave Revolts in the United States* (N.Y. 1939) pp.71, 72.

The earliest documented struggle of the African American Liberation Army against captivity occurred in 1526 in the area today known as South Carolina. One hundred of our ancestors revolted against the oppression of approximately 500 Spanish oppressors. Several Spaniards were killed and the Africans fled to the Indians for sanctuary.[11] Some Indian tribes provided both sanctuary and assistance by fighting alongside the African Liberation Army during our early struggles. The largest battles that the African American nation and the Seminole Indian nation joined as one force against the armies of the oppressive white nation were during the Seminole wars in Florida.

> On November 30, 1817, a group of Seminoles and blacks attacked a boat descending the Apalachicola River with supplies for the American outpost at Fort Scott in southern Georgia. Thirty-five American soldiers and the wives of six soldiers were killed in the assault; six soldiers and one woman were taken prisoner. The American public was infuriated by this "perfidious" Indian attack. In his message to Congress on March 25, 1818, President Monroe pointed to the "unprovoked" warfare of the Indians and charged that the Seminoles were bound by the 1796 treaty with the Creeks not to commit depredations against Americans. The regular army was authorized to prepare an invasion of Florida to punish the Seminoles."[12]

The coalition between our slave ancestors and the Seminoles was in contrast with the relationship they had with other tribes, notably, tribes such as the Choctaw, Cherokee Chickasaw, etc.,

---

[11] Ibid., pp.16, 17.
[12] Mary Frances Berry. *Black Resistance White Law* (N.Y. 1994) p.34.

because they were notorious slave owners,* and projected a master/slave relationship in their interactions with them.

The most noted battle against the oppressor nation occurred in August 1831. In this military blow against oppression, the African American Liberation Army under the leadership of Nat Turner killed sixty citizens of South Hampton, Virginia. The United States' government decided to use its might and crush the revolt and consequently,

> hundreds of soldiers, including cavalry and artillery units of the United States army swarmed over the county and together with the inhabitants, slaughtered over one hundred slaves".[13]

A citizen of the oppressor nation led the final recorded large-scale attack against the government and its forces of oppression before the Civil War. His name was John Brown and he led an interracial segment of the African American Liberation Army in an attack against our oppressors at Harper's Ferry, Virginia, in October 1859.[14]

THE CIVIL WAR

An attempt by the south to secede from the Union was the immediate cause of war within the oppressor nation itself. The South tried to secede because they wanted to compete with the industrialized North, using free slave labor. The white oppressor nation was almost torn asunder by this internal conflict. Both sides enlisted African American freemen and slaves to fight on their side. This war was not fought to free slaves, but to determine how the United States would advance economically.

---

* According to historical information, these tribes agreed to provide 40 acres to their freed slaves in some of their treaties with the USA government.
[13] Herbert Aptheker. *Negro Slave Revolts in the United States* (N.Y. 1939) p.50.
[14] See: W.E.B. DuBois. *John Brown* (N.Y.1956)

The relevance of the oppression and captivity of our ancestors was bound up with the free labor the Southern capitalists had access to. The war between the North and the South germinated in the contradiction of their economic interests.

JULY 1867-FRANKLYN TENNESSEE

Gunfire was exchanged between African American soldiers recently discharged from the Civil War and groups of ex-Confederate soldiers. One person was killed and fifty were wounded.

BLACK RECONSTRUCTION

An attempt was made to reconstruct the South. As reparation from the South to the North, plantations were confiscated, and many allotted to our ancestors who had given their free labor to cultivate them.

One scholar, Lerone Bennett claims the reactionary military forces of the oppressor overthrew reconstruction.

> The counterrevolution came to a head in 1876, the centennial of the Declaration of Independence. White men and black men in South Carolina, Louisiana and Florida fought small wars in 1876.[15]

This African American scholar classifies the violent clashes between African Americans and whites as "small wars." He does this because he understands on a historical level the definition of war.

DIS-ENFRANCHISEMENT

African Americans were finally allowed to vote. As a consequence, they were able to elect a few congressmen, a

---

[15] Lerone Bennett. *Confrontation: Black and White* (Baltimore, MD 1965) p.72.

lieutenant governor, and senators. Within ten years reconstruction was overthrown, our defenseless ancestors were left to protect themselves against the terror unleashed by new terrorist organizations sanctioned by the U.S. government.

> The Negro was deprived effectively of the franchise, of equality in compulsory public education and of protection against discrimination in the use of public facilities. The Negro did not succumb to this attack on his rights without a struggle. The use of wide-spread repression and the high incidence of violence against the Negro populace were, at least in part, the manifest expression of white reaction to Negro resistance. If Negroes had "known their place" it would not have been necessary to lynch Negroes in order to remind them of that "place".[16]

The conflict was a breeding ground of hate and fear. The ex-chattel slaves had to accommodate themselves to prescribed social and political roles or the white citizens would have slaughtered them. As Dr. Lerone Bennett claims, "There was also a great deal of talk in this period about a war of extermination,"[17] that white men were ready and waiting for black resistance against oppression, "so they could shoot them down like Indians, as a current phrase had it."[18]

1879 EXODUS FROM TYRANNY

Our ancestors claimed they migrated because of the crop lien and the prisoner-leasing systems, bad economic conditions, and the barrage of violent assaults perpetrated against them.

---
[16] Ibid.,
[17] Ibid. Bennett p.83.
[18] Ibid., p.84.

Bombings, fires, and lynchings were so prominent in the South that our ancestors fled to a safer haven in the North. However, as their numbers began to swell in the North, they found themselves on the defensive from attacks by the white northerners seemingly, because of labor competition. The northerners wasted no time in calling out their equivalence to the present day "W.A.R.," "Skin Heads," "K.K.K.," and their ilk.

> After the War there emerged a variety of vigilante groups, "Bald Knobbers" and similar quasi-bandit, quasi-legitimate, organizations that operated to keep the lid on social change and to attempt reinstatement of the "proper" superordinate-subordinate relationship that had occurred between whites and blacks in the antebellum South.[19]

BATTLE AT DANVILLE, VIRGINIA NOV 4, 1883

An African American allegedly bumped into a white man, and a small-scale battle took place lasting two days. When the smoke cleared, the casualties were one white person and four African Americans were dead, and four whites and six African Americans were wounded.

BATTLE IN TEXAS-COURT

The Supreme Court declared the Civil Rights Act of 1875 unconstitutional. This Act had provided for our ancestors' right to equal public accommodation. African Americans revolted in Gause, Texas, destroying property in the city. When our ancestors attempted to organize their labor to secure a $.25 raise in pay per day, the Governor ordered the state militia to force them from their homes on the old plantations. There was a

---

[19] Allen D. Grimshaw. *Racial Violence in the United States* (Chicago, IL:1969) p.37.

massacre of our ancestors by the oppressors' militia. Over 30 of them were killed.

LABOR STRIKE, LOUISIANA 1887

In 1880, when black workers on Louisiana sugar plantations went on strike to demand a wage increase from $.75 to $1.00 a day, the planters broke the strikes by calling up state militiamen who arrested the ringleaders for trespassing. By the fall of 1887, when wages were reduced to $.65 a day as a result of a poor crop in 1886, black workers, who had been unionized by the Knights of Labor, went on strike again, this time demanding $1.00 a day with rations and $1.25 without. When Governor Samuel D McEnery sent ten companies and two batteries of state militiamen to force the strikers to leave their homes on the plantations, a number of shooting incidents occurred, four blacks were killed and four whites wounded. In Thibodaux where hundreds of evicted blacks had gathered, the violence came to a head. .... Although the governor had withdrawn the militia a local judge, Taylor Beattie, declared martial law be enforced by troops of white vigilantes. Between the night of November 22 and noon the following day, thirty blacks were killed and hundreds of persons were wounded, of whom only two were white. The massacre ended the strike.[20]

In this battle the state militia was called out against the African Americans. These nearly defenseless people were forced from

---

[20] Mary Frances Berry. *Black Resistance White Law* (N.Y. 1994) p.88.

their homes, and approximately three-dozen of them were killed.

THE EAST ST. LOUIS BATTLE 1917[21]

"Many African Americans lost their lives as this battle raged and their 312 houses were set to the torch and burned during this confrontation."

HOUSTON TEXAS BATTLE 1917[22] A skirmish between white police and African American Military Police caused thirteen people to lose their lives, one was African American. Nineteen people were wounded and five were African American Military Police.

THE OMAHA BATTLE 1919[23] In Omaha, African American resistance to oppression led to the Lynching of one brother, and the partial destruction of the courthouse. The African Americans were well armed. It is reported that each of the 10,000 African American residents was armed. It took 700 Federal troops and a heavy electrical storm, to halt the uprising. This battle was so important that the Secretary of State became involved. He gave orders to General Leonard Wood, Commander of the Central Department of the Army, to go to Omaha and take charge of the situation.

By any definition, this was a state of war. The involvement of the Secretary of State and the Department of the Army qualifies it as such.

CHICAGO AT WAR 1919[24] African Americans and reactionary white groups battled in the streets, the governor

---

[21] Allen D. Grimshaw. *Racial Violence in the United States* (Chicago: 1969) pp.111-115.
[22] Ibid.,pp.73-87.
[23] Ibid.,pp92-94
[24] Ibid. Pp.87-91.

decided to quarantine the African American community. After 5 days the fighting stopped, with 38 known dead, 23 of these casualties were African Americans.

HARLEM 1935-1943[25]   This battle was essentially between our so-called, lower class brothers and sisters and the white police department.

THE DETROIT UPRISING, 1943[26]. Judge Edwards admitted in reporting to Commission investigators, there was "open warfare between the Detroit Negroes and the Detroit Police Department."

SOUTHERN U.S.A, 1963.   Suppression from reactionaries in Plaquemine, Louisiana, 150 African Americans were shocked with electric cattle prods, many children were hospitalized from kicks and being trampled by the horses the attacking policemen rode. Bombings were reported in Alabama, Arkansas, Florida, Georgia, Louisiana, Mississippi, South Carolina, and Virginia.

NEWARK UPRISING 1965[27]   "Over 75 cases of sniper fire were attributed to the African American community in this battle. This was a very destructive and expense ridden struggle."

WATTS UPRISING 1965[28]   The following were some of the reasons African Americans claimed for this battle:
1. To call attention to the African American problem.
2. Expression of African American hostility to Whites.
3. To serve an instrumental purpose of improving conditions, ending discrimination, or communicating to the "power structure".

---

[25] Ibid. Pp.117-128.
[26] Ibid. Pp.137-152.
[27] Tom Hayden. *Rebellion In Newark* (N.Y.1967)
[28] Robert Conot. *Rivers of Blood, Years of Darkness* (N.Y.1967)

This was one of the most devastating battles our people waged against the oppressive forces of America. Many consider this battle as the turning point of race relations in America.

DETROIT REBELLION 1967
Writer, John Hersey, described this uprising thusly:

> This episode contained all the mythic themes of racial strife in the United States: the arm of the law taking the law into its own hands; interracial sex; the subtle poison of racist thinking by 'decent' men who deny that they are racists; the societal limbo into which so many young black men have been driven ever since slavery, in our country; ambiguous justice in the courts; and the devastation in both black and white human lives that follow in the wake of violence.[29]

In this costly struggle 33 African Americans and 10 whites lost their lives.

The following is a major metropolitan newspaper report:

Detroit, July 27 (Thursday). – "Two National Guard tanks ripped a sniper's haven with machine guns Wednesday night and flushed out three shaggy-haired white youths. Snipers attacked a guard command post and Detroit's racial riot set a modern record for bloodshed. The death toll soared to 36, topping the Watts bloodbath of 1966 in which 35 died and making Detroit's insurrection the most deadly racial riot in modern U.S. history.

"In the attack on the sniper's nest, the Guardsmen poured hundreds of rounds of .50 caliber machine gunfire into the home, which authorities said housed arms and ammunition used by West Side sniper squads.

---

[29] John Hersey. *The Algiers Motel Incident* (N.Y. 1968) p.back cover.

"Guardsmen recovered guns and ammunition. A reporter with the troopers said the house, a neat brick home in a neighborhood of $20,000 to $50,000 homes, was torn apart by the machine gun and rifle fire.

"Sniper fire crackled from the home as the Guard unit approached. It was one of the first verified reports of sniping by whites.

"A pile of loot taken from riot-ruined stores was recovered from the sniper's haven, located ten blocks from the heart of the 200-square block riot zone. Guardsmen said the house had been identified as a storehouse of arms and ammunition for snipers. Its arsenal was regarded as an indication that the sniping or at least some of it was organized."

The newspaper articles archives at Tuskegee Institute indicate approximately 5,000 lynchings[30] of African American males and females between 1860 and 1960. The war goes on, with the police departments being the front line enforcer of policies for the oppressor nation. This attack against us is a fight to the finish and takes place constantly in every area of our lives. It is in its political form today and will remain so as long as it is expedient to remain so, but war and violence are always on the near horizon

Dorothy Benton-Lewis, a long time fighter for reparations claims:

> That the war continues can be seen in the persistent needs of the African community: decent affordable housing; food; medical and dental care; child- care, and relevant, quality education. The war can be seen in the continuing need for new bills - voting, civil, and human rights bills - year after year. It can be seen in the continual absence of job opportunities and of

---

[30] An excellent reference is: Ralph Ginzburg's, *100 Years of Lynchings* (Baltimore 1988).

meaningful jobs that pay a living wage that is fair and equal".[31]

Any serious consideration of the real problem (economic exploitation) confronting Black America must of necessity deal with our losses to the war that has been unjustly perpetrated against us for over 400 years, the horrific tortures during our captivity, our stolen labor, and our landlessness.

We must demand reparations for this unjust devastating war that is still being perpetrated against us. Germany can serve as our example of a country paying reparations for damages and losses inflicted in unjust wars. After the Germans were defeated, there were many debates about how much Germany could afford. Nevertheless, reparations were imposed on her to pay. Stephan A. Schuker, a professor of History at Brandeis University, explains one of the schedules of payments thusly:

> The 1921 London Schedule of Payments, which set forth Germany's formal obligations for the first time, demanded less than met the eye. The Supreme Council resolved the differences between the unrealistic expectations of the taxpaying public in allied countries and the actual capacity of Germany to pay through artful obfuscation. The reparation Commission had not found it possible (in part because of British foot dragging) to collect the statistical information that would allow a scientific determination of Berlin's treaty liability. It's finding that Germany owed 132 milliard gold marks (in round numbers $33 billion) therefore reflected a measure of rough political justice. Still, the figure was not an unreasonable first approximation of damages. Moreover, the

---

[31] Dorthy Lewis-Benton. *Black Reparations Now*. (Baltimore MD 1990) p.22.

Supreme Allied Council agreed to divide the nominal total into segments. Germany would have to pay interest and amortization on two bond series totaling only 50 milliard gold marks. That represented the essential burden implied by the London Schedule.[32]

In the end it was the United States government paying reparations to Germany by allowing her to default on loan payments, etc., to offset the cost of the reparations. The why of the turn of events is not germane to this report. What is important is that Germany was mandated to pay reparations for the losses caused by the wars she instigated. Europeans have been and still are involved in an unjust war against Africans. Are we any less human than those who suffered losses because of Germany's attacks against them?

Yes, our people have struggled and defended themselves every step of the way in this war. We fought when they attacked our Motherland (Africa). We struggled and revolted aboard those cargo ships, on the plantations, and we still struggle to defend ourselves from attacks in our urban ghettos.

We deserve reparations for our losses from the war battles that have been waged against us for the last 500 years. We must demand payment from the Europeans, Americans, and their governments.

---

[32] Stephen A. Schuker. *American "Reparations" to Germany* (Princeton, NJ. 1988) p.16.

Chapter 2

CAPTIVES OF WAR

America is composed of two nations (in conflict), one white, rich, powerful, privileged and oppressive, and the other black, poor, powerless, captive victim of war, and oppressed. These two nations are separate and unequal, and in imagery representative of master and slave. The same dynamics that maintained that relationship during chattel slavery still exist today. These two nations have been embraced in conflict with one another since the beginning of the Atlantic slave trade. Sometimes the conflict has been violently intense and destructive of lives and property. While at others less so. However, at all times it has been focused through and influenced by the prism of racism. This prism is constructed of various facets; one informs the white nation that it is pure, and the black nation evil. Granted, this basic belief has motivated the white oppressor to act with impunity against our black nation for several centuries. However, it was the motivation for profits that was the canon that fired the shot, which started and maintained the Atlantic slave trade wars against Africa and its descendants.

A careful analysis of our African American nation's situation relative to the general American context will inform us that we are controlled economically, educationally, politically, socially, and above all, militarily by others. In other words, we are a captive nation. We are the captives of war held in bondage by our captors and consequently have no citizen rights the captors are bound to respect. This doesn't mean we currently cannot move around in or leave America. It does mean we are a people who were captured in an unjust war and transported to the Americas and other foreign lands to give our free labor for centuries while in captivity. For instance, while in chattel slavery, our people worked from "sun-up to sun-down", providing profits for the plantation owners while receiving the whip regularly and only the bare resources necessary for survival. Their owners main concern was how much profit could be extracted from their lives before they were used up. This is still their primary concern today.

To justify the degradation they subjected us to, required a philosophy that would depict us as being a lower link in Darwin's theory of evolution and consequently their burden. This burden would entail delivering us from our "savage state", and uplifting us towards their "civilized state." Consequently, modern racism had its origin and served as the tool of justification for the inhuman treatment of our people. Modern racism isn't and never has been the problem itself, but has been used to provide justification to the racist for his actions that sustains the problem. The problem is the contradiction (conflict) between the captive Black Nation and the privileged White Nation and its government.

Thomas E. Watson, leader of the populist movement prior to becoming an open critic and enemy of the African American Nation, recognized this contradiction as early as 1892 when he wrote:

> ...Never before did two distinct races dwell together under such conditions. And the problem is can these two races, distinct in color, distinct in social life, and distinct as political powers, dwell together in peace and prosperity. Upon a question so difficult and delicate no man should

> dogmatize - nor dodge. The issue is here; grows more urgent every day, and must be met.[33]

The urgency of a solution to this problem was begged for because if allowed to remain unresolved could only bring about a future confrontation that would involve and destroy the total country. Watson claims that after,

> Having given this subject much anxious thought my opinion is that the future happiness of the two races will never be assured until the political motives, which drive them asunder, into two distinct and hostile factions, can be removed.[34]

So here we are today, a colonized captive nation within a nation controlled by laws, which are enforced by the white nation's local foot soldiers, the police departments.

Kenneth Clark succinctly describes our condition as a captive and colonized nation within the United States:

> Ghettoes are the consequence of the imposition of external power and the institutionalization of powerlessness. In this respect, they are in fact social, political, educational, and above all- economic colonies. Those confined within the ghetto walls are subject peoples. They are victims of the greed, cruelty, insensitivity, guilt and fear of their masters.[35]

Our ancestors were not captured and enslaved to serve for racism's sake but rather for the sake of economics. Racism was/is merely a philosophical and ideological tool used to

---
[33] Thomas E. Watson. The *Negro Question in the South*. 1892 Pp.540-550
[34] Ibid. Pp.540-550
[35] Kenneth Clark. *Youth in the Ghetto* (N.Y. 1964) p.10.

justify our ancestors' enslavement and our continued oppression for profits while providing a clear conscience for our oppressors. In practice it was used to maintain chattel enslavement of our ancestors and currently to maintain our present neo-enslavement.

Many of our African American brothers and sisters find it hard to comprehend how White Americans could wage a revolution for their liberation from England while keeping our ancestors in bondage. What they fail to realize is that the struggle between America and England was really a,

> ...Decision of the white capitalist classes of North America to break their colonial bondage to Great Britain and strike out on their own as an independent capitalist nation.[36]

Our ancestors were the resource tools the capitalist class owned and used to expand their profits. Now please ask yourselves, would you voluntarily give up your profit-making tool? Of course not and neither would they. There was no contradiction in their logic when they fought for their separation from England while holding us in bondage. They wanted to separate so they could develop as an independent capitalist country and we as their free labor played a prominent role in their economic dreams of profits. Besides the general opinion among the white population (even their leaders) was the inferiority of our people.[37] Their theology indicated our ancestors deserved enslavement because God had ordained it through Noah's curse on Ham's descendents.

Racism has become an integral part of the national character of the white nation, and is deeply embedded in its psyche and

---

[36] Robert Allen. *A Historical Synthesis: Black Liberation and World Revolution.* Black Scholar. vol.3 San Francisco, 1976.

[37] See Part IV in this book. *The Land Issue*, Thomas Jefferson, John C. Calhoun and Samuel Cartwright express their beliefs and attitudes towards African Americans.

outward institutions. Racism is a white mental problem and as much as some of us (black folk) desire to solve it we can't. Albert Memmi advises us that,

> Before taking root in the individual, racism has taken root in the institutions and ideologies all around him, in the education he receives and the culture he acquires.[38]

Trying to resolve the issue of racism is similar to unraveling the skin from an onion seeking its essence and consequently, wasting time that could be better utilized in seeking ways to help us become re-developed, self-sufficient, liberated people. Besides only white people can resolve white racism. If we were to radically redefine ourselves, we would simultaneously redraw the archaic racist boundaries that define the racist. When they are forced by circumstance or otherwise to realize it is in their best interest to eradicate racism, they will.

The primary function of any oppressed people is to seek liberation from what oppresses them. The Bible teaches us to resist the devil. Therefore our struggle is and always has been against whatever prevents us from being what God designed and desires us to be. Racism is a white problem that informs the white racist that people of African descent are uncivilized heathens and it is morally right to do whatever it takes to civilize them. Consequently, racists go all over the world in confidence of their rightness and weighed down in war resources and impose their will upon the nations of the world. But we must be ever mindful of the fact that they cannot succeed as the great oppressors in our lives unless we decide to allow them to.

We are a captive nation whose utility within the capitalist system is to provide profits for the investors. Our role as profit

---

[38] Albert Memmi. *Dominated Man*. (Boston 1968) p.196.

producers is almost exhausted and we are rapidly becoming a drain on profits. This is an awful condition to be in when the controlling capitalist nation is motivated by profits. We are colonial subjects and until we recognize this we will never solve the problem we are struggling against. As Eldredge Cleaver tried to impress on us in 1968:

> Black people are a stolen people held in a colonial status on stolen land, and any analysis which does not acknowledge the colonial status of black people cannot hope to deal with the real problem.[39]

The question of how to liberate our captive selves within our captors own political homeland is the question we should deal with, not how to end racism. Racism could end tomorrow and have no positive economic advantage for us.

---

[39] Eldredge Cleaver. The *Land Question*. *Ramparts*, vol. 6 (N.Y. 1968) p.51.

Chapter 3

STOLEN LABOR

PRIOR TO 1865

This is the period when members of the black nation were considered as commodities, or properties of their owners (white nation) and dehumanized in the master's mind. Worst of all many of our ancestors internalized their dehumanization. As such, they existed solely for the economic benefit of these owners. A lot of profit was extracted from their lives under the system of slavery. It was derived from the sales of our ancestors and from their stolen labor. Our ancestors paid a heavy price with their forced contributions to the white nation's economic advancements.

The sale of our ancestors had many participants. Europeans, Arabs, Africans, and Americans all made profits from these sales. In Africa, some chiefs and black traders were heavily involved in the trading of their own people. How could a chief involve himself in the sale of his own people? Very simply stated, the white man had goods such as beads, bracelets, jingling bells, and brandy from France,[40] which the chief and his people wanted. Many of the economic systems of the West Coast were based on this trade. The people wanted the white man's merchandise and the white man wanted captives in trade for his goods. If a chief decided to quit the trade, the white men would provide some other tribe with arms and resources to

---

[40] Anne Terry White. Hum*an Cargo* (Champaign, IL 1972) p.34.

attack the chief and his people and march them off into slavery. A chief who found himself involved in the trade was caught in a "catch 22 situation," "damned if you do, damned if you don't." He became trapped in the system.

In any event, the chiefs involved in the trade made profits, as did the African traders. One black trader named Ben Johnson was so prolific at capturing and selling his brothers and sisters that those in the trade nicknamed him 'Grand Trading Man from Wappoa.' It is rather ironic that this same trader eventually found himself aboard a slave ship chained to another slave he had sold to a ship's captain.

In a period of just ten years, from 1783 to 1793, Liverpool slave merchants utilizing 878 ships transported over 300,000 of our ancestors across the seas and oceans.

> ... At a value of £15,186,850. Deductions for various commissions, and other charges, gave Liverpool a gross return of $12,294,116, or £1,700,000 per year. After all necessary expenses in transporting and insurance were calculated, it was estimated that there was gain of 30% on every slave sold.[41]

Slaving was so profitable in Liverpool England, that over 50% of all its shipping was engaged in transporting captured Africans.

When those captives who survived the horrid Middle Passage arrived at their destination, they were sold again on the Auction Block. Everyone made profits, that is, everyone but our captive ancestors. Mostly, they received oppression and the whip.

The function of a slave plantation was to make a profit in agriculture. It was reasonable that free labor should yield more

---

[41] Frank Tannenbaum. *Slave & Citizen* (N.Y. 1946) pp.17,18.

profit than contracted labor, especially if the slaves' upkeep expenses were kept to the bare minimum.[42] If stolen slave labor had not been very profitable it would not have proliferated or lasted so long.

> Slavery was above all a labor system. Wherever in the South the master lived, however many slaves he owned, it was his bondsmen's productive capacity that he generally valued most. And to the problem of organizing and exploiting their labor with maximum efficiency he devoted much of his attention.[43]

Whether the slave labor produced profits for the slave master or not is not really relevant to whether our ancestors' labor was stolen or not. However, with some plantations it was very profitable.

> The slaves on the rice plantations of the Waccamaw made their masters wealthy. Since the vast All Saints rice plantations were largely self sufficient, much of the planters' income from the sale of rice was clear profit. Ward was described as making $360 clear to every hand that hoes.[44]

The profitableness of stolen labor is not the core issue here, what is of central importance is whether our ancestors were deprived of the immediate product of their labor. Any sound

---

[42] *Black People and the U.S. Economy.* Our *Case for Reparations.* Burning Spear Publications. Oakland, CA.
This publication claims, "The maintenance cost of the slave according to the owners' estimate was $20.00 per year for a field hand, which he was expected to produce and surpass by the time he was 9 years old." p.60.
[43] Kenneth Stamp. *The Pecular Institution* (NY. 1956) p.34.
[44] Charles Joyner. Down *by the Riverside.* (Chicago, IL 1985) p.33

thinking person must admit that the masters controlled the slaves' labor. It was the master who exploited their labor for his profits. Because of this deprivation, this loss of our ancestor's natural God given wealth (labor), we have entered into the world of the millennium without the fruits of that inheritance. The slave masters' children and institutions have inherited our wealth. The United States government and Europe owe the descendents of slaves their inheritance, plus accumulated interest for their stolen labor.

The inheritance of the fruits of labor of the ancestors was so important that detailed statues were instituted by Moses to be obeyed by the people. These laws were put in place to make sure that a blood-related individual would receive his or her rightful inheritance.*

> 1. Then came the daughters of Zelophehad, the son of Hepher the son of Gilead, the son of Machir, the son of Manasseh, of the families of Manasseh the son of Joseph: and these are the names of his daughters; Mahlah, Noah, and Hoglah, and Milcah, and Tirzah:
> 2. And they stood before Moses, and before Eleazar the priest, and before the princes and all the congregation, by the door of the tabernacle of the congregation, saying,
> 3. Our father died in the wilderness, and he was not in the company of them that gathered themselves together against the LORD in the company of Korah; but died in his own sin, and had no sons.
> 4. Why should the name of our father be done away from among his family, because he hath no

---

* See *Exodus* 3:22. "Every woman shall borrow (demand according to the Hebrew word) from the Egyptian women, all her friends and visitors gold, silver and clothing". They were not to use this compensation for themselves but were to give it as an *inheritance* to their sons and daughters.

son? Give unto us therefore a possession among the brethren of our father.

5. And Moses brought their cause before the LORD.

6. And the LORD spake unto Moses, saying,

7. The daughters of Zelophehad speak right: thou shalt surely give them a possession of an inheritance among their father's brethren; and thou shalt cause the inheritance of their father to pass unto them.

8. And thou shall speak unto the children of Israel saying, If a man die, and have no son, then ye shall cause his inheritance to pass unto his daughter. And if he has no daughter, then ye shall give his inheritance unto his brethren.

10. And if he has no brethren, then ye shall give his inheritance unto his father's brethren.

11. And if his father have no brethren, then ye shall give his inheritance unto his kinsman that is next to him of his family and he shall possess it: and it shall be unto the children of Israel a statute of judgment, as the LORD commanded Moses.[45]

The above right of inheritance statue was given by Moses and focused on the material inheritance. Traditionally, the oldest son was the inheritor of the fruits of the ancestors. However, Moses changed the law so that a female could inherit if there was no son. That's how important it is for descendents to receive the fruits of their ancestor's labor. As descendents they are the rightful heirs.

Jesus Christ promised us that if we accepted Him as our Lord and Savior, we would be co-inheritors with Him and have eternal life.

---

[45] *Numbers.* 27:1-11.

> 28...Verily I say unto you, that ye which have followed me, in there generation when the Son of man shall sit in the throne of glory, ye also shall sit upon thrones, judging the twelve of Israel.
> 29 And every one that hath forsaken houses or brethren, or sisters, or father, or mother, or wife, or children, or lands, my name's sake, shall receive an hundred-fold, and shall inherit everlasting life.
> 30 But many that are first shall be last; and the last shall be first.[46]

The Judeo/Christian stream of religious thought emphasizes the rights of physical and spiritual inheritance of descendants. The inheritance of the Kingdom of God results from our adoption into His Holy Family. We become his children and brothers and sisters of Jesus Christ and consequently co-inheritors with Jesus. Our inheritance includes the kingdom of heaven and all of God's spiritual treasures.

So as we see, inheritance played an important role in the Old Testament and the New Testament of Jesus Christ. Where is our physical inheritance of the labors of our ancestors? It is rightfully ours and whoever stole our inheritance reminds one of the stealing from Esau of his inheritance by birthright. We have an inheritance that was stolen and we must use our God-given right and demand the return our stolen inheritance by those who stole it, provided for its theft, or have been given privileged use of it for nearly 400 years.

STOLEN LABOR SINCE 1865

During the period of neo-slavery 1865 to the present, we have continued to struggle against that which oppresses us. After chattel slavery came to an end, a new form of slavery was

---

[46] *Matthew.* 19:28-30.

put in place. Under this system of peonage, many of our ancestors were kept on plantations where the stealing of their labor was ongoing, even after the Emancipation Proclamation. According to Carl Schurz,

> "Some planters held back their former slaves on their plantations by brute force. Armed bands of white men patrolled the county roads to drive back the Negroes wandering about. Dead bodies of murdered Negroes were found on and near the highways and byways. Gruesome reports came from the hospitals - reports of colored men and women whose ears had been cut off, whose skulls had been broken by blows, whose bodies had been slashed by knives or lacerated with scourges. A number of such cases, I had occasioned to examine myself. A veritable reign of terror prevailed in many parts of the South.[47]

African American labor continued to be stolen for many years after emancipation. The above is evidence of some former masters' refusal to cease this practice.

Several states began to concoct laws that were exploitative of the newly freed black workers. These laws were designed to replace the slave laws and were a synthesis of the slavery statutes, apprenticeship, vagrancy and West Indian Laws relative to emancipated slaves. In reality these codes were very oppressive and served as a step back into slavery. The following samples indicate their intent to exploit our ancestors and the advantages allowed to the exploiters to steal their labor. Several states had a set of these oppressive "Black Codes" whose real purpose appeared as a legal way of stealing our ancestors' labor. The following are some examples:

---

[47] 39th Congress, 1st Session, Senate Executive Documents No. 2, Report of Carl Schurz.

MISSISSIPPI APPRENTICE LAW[48]

"Sec.1. It shall he the duty of all sheriffs, justices of the pence, and other civil officers of the several counties in this State, to report to the probate courts of their respective counties semi-annually, at the January and July terms of said courts, all freedmen, free negroes, and mulattoes, under the age of eighteen, in their respective counties, beats or districts, who are orphans, or whose parent or parents have not the means or who refuse to provide for and support said miners; and thereupon it shall be the duty of said probate court to order the clerk of said court to apprentice said miners to some competent and suitable person, on such terms as the court may direct, having a particular care to the interest of said minor: Providing, that the former owner of said miners shall have the preference when, in the opinion of the court, he or she shall be a suitable person for that purpose.

Sec. 2. The said court shall be fully satisfied that the person or persons to whom said minor shall be apprenticed shall be a suitable person to have the charge and care of said minor, and fully to protect the interest of said minor. The said court shall require the said master or mistress to execute bond and security, payable to the State of Mississippi, conditioned that he or she shall furnish said minor with sufficient food and clothing; to treat said minor humanely; furnish medical attention in case of sickness; teach, or cause to be taught, him or her to read and write. if under fifteen years old, and will conform to any law that may be hereafter passed for the regulation of the duties and relation of master and apprentice.

Sec.3. In the management and control of said apprentice, said master or mistress shall have the Dower to inflict such moderate corporal chastisement as a father or guardian is allowed to

---

[48] Ibid., Pp.152-154

inflict on his or her child or ward at common law: Provided, that in no case shall cruel or inhuman punishment be inflicted.

Sec. 4. If any apprentice shall leave the employment of his or her master or mistress, without his or her consent, said master or mistress may pursue and recapture said apprentice, and bring him or her before any justice of the peace of the county, whose duty it shall be to remand said apprentice to the service of his or her master or mistress; and in the (b) Mississippi, 1865 event of a refusal on the part of said apprentice so to return, then said justice shall commit said apprentice to the jail of said county, on failure to give bond, to the next term of the county court; and it shall be the duty of said court at the first term thereafter to investigate said case, and if the court shall be of opinion that said apprentice left the employment of his or her master or mistress without good cause, to order him or her to be punished, as provided for the punishment of hired freedmen, as may be from time to time provided for by law for desertion, until he or she shall agree to return to the service of his or her master or mistress:....if the court shall believe that said apprentice had good cause to quit his said master or mistress, the court shall discharge said apprentice from said indenture, and also enter a judgment against the master or mistress for not more than one hundred dollars, for the use and benefit of said apprentice."

SHARE CROPPING

So-called Reconstruction (black power) was in effect until 1879, under the protection of black militias. But the betrayal of the northern industrialists and liberals prevented the consolidation of their freedom and independence. African Americans were driven off freely held land and back into a system of share-cropping in which each year of stolen labor produced crops for the increasing profits of the landowners. Under this system white landowners furnished land, shelter, seed, and farming implements to our ancestors, who supplied the labor to grow and harvest the crop. The General store advanced credit for food, clothing, and other needs at exorbitant interest rates. Gunnar Myrdal reports the following observation about thievery under this system

> The "advancing" of food, clothing, and other necessities of life is a significant part of the system. Since the tenant is ordinarily without resources--otherwise he would not be a tenant--he cannot usually wait for his wages until the crop has been harvested and sold. He has, therefore, to live on a credit basis at least during a large part of the year. For an average period of seven months, according to Woofter's sample study for 1934, the tenant receives credit from the landlord, often in a special store or commissary, where he can buy household supplies up to a certain amount a month. This amount varies according to the size of the family, the prospects for the crop, the market conditions, and so on. The average in Woofter's sample was $12.80 per month and $88 per year."' A study of the Yazoo-Mississippi Delta in 1936 showed an average subsistence advance per year of about $94 for sharecroppers and $138 for share tenants. If operating credit is included, the amounts were $162 and $283, respectively.
>
> The interest rates charged for these advances are extremely high. A flat rate of 10 per cent is usual but, since the duration of the credit is only a few months, the annual rate is several times higher. According to Woofter's sample study in '934, it was no less than 37 per cent."" A plantation study for 1937 on a somewhat smaller sample gave almost the same average. These rates

were two to three times as high as those paid by the operators (landlords) for short-term credit.[49]

This system was so orchestrated by the masters that 59% of these share-croppers ended up year after year deeper in debt to the landowner, and 17 percent of them cleared nothing, and 25 percent cleared $1600 or less for an entire year of slave labor. It is evident that someone made a lot of profits from this stolen labor, high interest rates for credit and overpriced products.

CHAIN GANGS

The unemployed ex-slaves were often picked up for vagrancy and imprisoned. While imprisoned they were used to construct the basic infrastructures and they were leased out to the agricultural businesses which made big profits from their stolen labor.

> In addition, African people were arrested at any time and charged with "vagrancy," which simply meant being poor. Huge-chain gangs were made up of such "vagrants" and were used to build roads and levees, clear forests and drain swamps. Through the systems of chain gangs and sharecropping, owner-ship of African labor power was transferred from individual slave owners to the agricultural companies, and states".[50]

The following is a copy of a section of one of those laws for your information and enlightenment. It clearly illustrates how and why the laws were created. They were made specifically

---

[49] Gunnar Myrdal. *An American Dilemma.* Vol 1, (N.Y. 1944) p.247.
[50] African people Socialist Party. *Black People and the U.S. Economy.* Burning Spear. (Oakland, CA. 1982) p.61.

for, and implemented to entrap poor black people and exploit their labor.

CHAIN GANG LABOR LAW

Sec. 5. If any freedman, free negro, or mulatto, convicted of any of the misdemeanors provided against in this act, shall fail or refuse for the space of five days, after conviction, to pay the fine and costs imposed, such person shall be hired out by the sheriff or other officer, at public outcry, to any white person who will pay said fine and all costs, and take said convict for the shortest time.

The perpetual theme has been the continuous historical flow of white grand theft of black labor in the past down to the presence.

MODERN PRISON SYSTEMS

It has been claimed by various authorities that over one-third of African American males between the ages of 18 to 35 are either in, or associated with the penal system. Well over 50% of all prison inmates are African Americans. Something is wrong with this system especially, since African Americans are only 12% of the population. The prison system is nothing more for African American males than an extension of the slave plantation.

The prison system has its slave drivers and exploits the labor and dignity of prisoners. There appears to be three functions to the prison system: 1. remove certain people out of society, 2. revenge, and 3. economic exploitation. By 1991 this industry was at $37 billion and growing.[51] There is a continuity of historical flow from the prison system back through the chain gangs (free labor), to the plantations.

---

[51] Clarence J. Munford. *Race And Reparations* (Trenton, N.J. 1996) p.325.

MODERN WAGES AND BUSINESS

When white workers are paid a certain amount for performing a specific job and a black person performs the same job and is paid less, the difference between their wages represent theft of labor.

> It is estimated that the difference in wages paid out annually to white and black working people amount to over $27 billion. In the automobile industry, for instance, somewhere around 150,000 black workers make $7,200 a year or less –the poverty level. This is accomplished by a system of job classifications which places 121,000 of them in the three lowest categories. If the auto corporations were forced to pay them an additional $800 a year which would raise their wages to the annual average for the industry (1970) it would raise the wage bill for the industry giants $120,000,000 a year.[52]

The auto industry stole African American workers' labor at the tune of over $120,000,000 a year.

The 1970 median income for white citizens was $36,494. Black descendents of slaves' income for the same period was $21,330. A theft of over $15,000 exploited from each black worker. This is grand theft of African American labor. For those of us who are under the illusion that things are getting better, as recently as 1992 the theft of our labor increased to $19,260. The income of whites increased to $40,421 and black income decreased to $21,161. This was a net loss of $161 since 1970 for each black worker. Where is the so-called economic progress?

---

[52] Carl Boice. *Black Labor is Black Power*. *Black Scholar*. Vol.2 Num.2 (San Francisco 1970) pp.29, 30.

We also suffer greatly economically because of discrimination in the job market. We have developed a proverbial saying, "We are the last hired, and the first fired", to capture and illustrate this reality.

Andrew Hacker informs us on the plight of the black worker and unemployment in the United States.

> The capitalist system has been frank in admitting that it cannot always create jobs for everyone who wants to work. This economic reality has certainly been a pervasive fact of black life. For as long as records have been kept, in good times and bad, white America has ensured that the unemployment imposed on blacks will be approxi-mately double that experienced by whites stated very simply, if you are black in America, you will find it at least twice as hard to find or keep a job.[53]

Some economic thinkers claim it takes a 4%-6% unemployment rate to keep capitalism healthy and maintain surplus growth. It is a documented fact that our people suffer disproportionately. Our orchestrated unemployment rate is double that of white Americans.

---

[53] Andrew Hacker. *Two Nations: Black and White, Separate, Hostile, Unequal.* (N.Y. 1995) p. 108.

Chapter 4

CRIMES AGAINST BLACK HUMANITY

ON THE CARGO SHIPS

The horrendous nature of all aspects of the infamous Atlantic slave trade is well known and documented. Nearly 100 million people were kidnapped placed in chains and shipped across the oceans in the humid, stench filled, rat infested, disease-ridden holds of cargo ships. There are claims that only 20 million made it to the various destinations. Eighty million lost their lives during the marches from the interior to the coast, in the slave forts and during transit on ships across the oceans.

Rev. John Newton, the Captain of one of those ships that transported the captive Africans, informs us of the size of the room down in the ship's hold the captives were packed in.

> The cargo of a vessel of a hundred tons or a little more is calculated to purchase from 220 to 250 slaves. Their lodging rooms below the deck which are three (for the men, the boys and the women) besides a place for the sick, are sometimes more than five feet high and sometimes less; and this height is divided toward the middle for the slaves lie in two rows, one above the other, on each side of the ship, close to each other like books upon a shelf. I have known

> them so close that the shelf would not easily contain one more.[54]

These captives however, should consider themselves fortunate, if the hold had been six feet deep instead of five feet another shelf would have been added in which case each captive would have had less than twenty inches of head room.

Our imaginations cannot fathom the depths of despair and the anxieties such closeness must have elicited from the emotions of these poor souls who had been snatched from their families and forcibly separated from them forever. Can you imagine how many of them drifted into the realm of insanity or death to escape the pain and brokenness they felt? Captain John Newton adds:

> The poor creatures, thus cramped, are likewise in irons for the most part, which makes it difficult for them to turn or move or attempt to rise or to lie down without hurting themselves or each other. Every morning, perhaps, more instances than one are found of the living and the dead fastened together.[55]

There was constant quarrelling and struggling amongst the captives in the darkness of the ship holds at night as they stumbled over each other while shackled together, trying to get to the waste deposit buckets supplied for their bowel release.

> In each of the apartments are placed three or four large buckets, of a conical form, nearly two feet in diameter at the bottom and only one foot at the top and in depth about twenty-eight inches, to

---

[54] John Newton. *Thoughts Upon the African Slave Trade* (London 1788)
[55] Alexander Falcolnbridge. *An Account of the Slave Trade on the Coast of Africa* (London 1788)

> which, when necessary, the negroes have recourse. It often happens that those who are placed at a distance from the buckets, in endeavoring to get to them, tumble over their companions, in consequence of their being shackled. These accidents, although unavoidable, are productive of continual quarrels in which some of them are always bruised. In this situation, unable to proceed and prevented from going to the tubs, they desist from the attempt; and as the necessities of nature are not to be resisted. They ease themselves as they lie.[56]

The captives often stopped trying to make it to the buckets and surrendered to the call of nature and released their bowels where they were. If they were packed on top, this filth splashed down on the person below. Can you imagine the confusion this caused? They slept in this filth and ate their meager meals with their filth-infested hands. It is no wonder disease was so rampant on those cargo ships.

It was horrible when the weather was fair but when the weather changed and wind and rain came sickness and death increased. A ship's surgeon, Dr. Alexander Falcolnbridge, informs us with eyewitness account information of the horror in the ship holds during heavy rains.

> Some wet and blowing weather having occasioned the port-holes to be shut and the grating to be covered, fluxes and fevers among the negroes ensued. While they were in this situation, I frequently went down among them till at length their rooms became so extremely hot as to be only bearable for a very short time.

---
[56] Ibid.

> But the excessive heat was not the only thing that rendered their situation intolerable. The deck, that is, the floor of their rooms, was so covered with the blood and mucus, which had proceeded from them in consequence of the flux, that it resembled a slaughter house... Numbers of the slaves having fainted they were carried upon deck where several of them died and the rest with great difficulty were restored.[57]

Many captives were jettisoned overboard to save the investors their profits. Insurance companies paid for jettisoned slaves but restricted payments for captives who died on board. One of the most famous cases of captives being thrown overboard into the ocean occurred on a ship named Zong. This ship sailed out of Liverpool, England. The Commanding Officer, Captain Collingswood, ordered over 100 sick captives to be thrown overboard.

> The said Luke Collingswood picked, or caused to be picked out, from the cargo of the same ship, one hundred and thirty-three slaves, all or most of whom were sick or weak, and not likely to live; and ordered the crew by turns to throw them into the sea; which most inhuman order was cruelly complied with.[58]

Captain John Newton informs us of how, when the voyage was coming to its end, they would take the irons off the captives, feed them well, oil their bodies, and a sense of freedom in-filled their wretched selves but,

---

[57] Ibid., Falcolnbridge.
[58] Quoted in: *Black Cargoes* (N.Y. 1967) pp. 125, 126.

> This joy is short-lived indeed. The condition of the unhappy slaves is in a continual progress from bad to worse ... perhaps they would wish to spend the remainder of their days on ship-board, could they know beforehand the nature of the servitude which awaits them on shore; and that the dreadful hardships and sufferings they have already endured would, to the most of them, only terminate in excessive toil, hunger and the excruciating tortures of the cart-whip, inflicted at the caprice of an unfeeling overseer, proud of the power allowed him of punishing whom, and when, and how he pleases.[59]

So many of our ancestors lost their lives to the ocean, that hungry sharks would follow the ships from the coasts of Africa to coasts of destination.

DURING CHATTEL SLAVERY

The following document comes from the pen of a citizen of the white oppressor nation:

> As SLAVEHOLDERS AND their apologists are volunteer witnesses In their own cause, and are flooding the world with testimony that their slaves are kindly treated; that they are well fed, well clothed, well housed, well lodged, moderately worked... and bountifully provided with all things needful for their comfort. We propose - first, to disprove their assertions by the testimony of a multitude of impartial witnesses, and then to put slave-holders themselves through a course of cross-questioning which shall draw

---

[59] John Newton, *Thoughts Upon the African Slave Trade* (London 1788).

their condemnation out of their own mouths. We will prove that the slaves in the United States are treated with barbarous inhumanity; that they are overworked, underfed, wretchedly clad and lodged, and have insufficient sleep; that they are often made to wear round their necks iron collars armed With prongs, to drag heavy chains and weights at their feet while working in the field, and to wear yokes, and bells, and iron horns; that they are often kept confined in the stocks day and night for weeks together, made to wear gags in their mouths for hours or days, have some of their front teeth torn out or broken off, that they may be easily detected when they run away; that they are frequently flogged with terrible severity, have red pepper rubbed into their lacerated flesh, and hot brine, spirits of turpentine, &c., poured over the gashes to increase the torture; that they are often stripped naked, their backs and limbs cut with knives, bruised and mangled by scores and hundreds of blows with the paddle, and terribly torn by the claws of cats, drawn over them by their tormentors: that they are often hunted with blood hounds and shot down like beasts, or torn in pieces by dogs; that they are often suspended by the arms and whipped and beaten till they faint, and when revived by restoratives, beaten again till they faint, and sometimes till they die; that their ears are often cut off, their eyes knocked out, their bones broken, their flesh branded with red hot irons; that they are maimed, mutilated and burned to death over slow fires.[60]

---

[60] Theodore Weld, *Introduction to American Antislavery. American Slavery as It is.* (N.Y. 1839) pp. 9-10.

African scholar of the Diaspora, C.L.R. James reports the following tortures in the Caribbean Islands.

> There was no ingenuity that fear or a depraved imagination could devise which was not employed to break their spirit and satisfy the lusts and resentment of their owners and guardians–irons on the hands and feet, blocks of wood that the slaves had to drag behind them wherever they went, the tin plate mask designed to prevent the slaves eating the sugar-cane, the iron collar. Whipping was interrupted in order to pass a piece of hot wood on the buttocks of the victim; salt, pepper, citron, cinders, aloes, and hot ashes were poured on the bleeding wounds.[61]

The slaves received extreme punishment and sometimes the master thought the whipping wasn't enough and used whatever techniques and ingredients to aggravate the painful wounds. Often they were whipped to death. C.L.R. James adds:

> Mutilations were common, limbs, ears, and sometimes the private parts, to deprive them of the pleasures that they could indulge in without expense. Their masters poured burning wax on their arms and hands and shoulders, emptied the boiling cane sugar over their heads, burned them alive, roasted them over slow fires, filled them with gunpowder and blew them up with a match; buried them up to the neck and smeared their heads with sugar that the flies might devour them; fastened them near to nests of ants and

---

[61] C.L.R. James. *The Black Jacobins* (N.Y. 1962) p. 12.

wasps: made to eat their excrement, drink their urine, and lick the saliva of other slaves.[62]

I have read accounts of the horrible treatment of Jews in the concentration camps of Europe. I have never read or heard however, of any torture and horror visited upon any group of persons in history over so long a period of time comparable to the hell our ancestors suffered.

POST CIVIL WAR VIOLENCE
Examples:
1. Sam Davis hung by mob in Harrodsburg, May 28, 1868.
2. Several persons were ordered to leave their homes at Standford, KY. Aug. 7, 1868.
3. Silas Woodford age sixty badly beaten by disguised mob. Mary Smith Curtis and Margaret Mosby were also badly beaten, near Keene Jessemine, County August 1868.
4. James Parker killed by Ku Klux Pulaski, Aug.1868
5. Attack on Negro cabin in Spencer, County - a woman outraged Dec. 1868.
6. Ku Klux whipped boy at Standford, March 12, 1869.
7. Chas Henderson shot & his wife killed by mob on silver creek Madison, County, July 1869.
8. Ku Klux attacked Frank Searcy house in Madison, County man shot, November 1869.
9. Searcy hung by mob Madison, County at Richmond, Nov.1869.
10. Ku Klux killed Robbert Mershon daughter shot, Nov. 1869.
11. Two Negroes killed by mob while in civil custody near Mayfield Graves County Dec. 1869.
12. Allen Cooper killed by Ku Klux in Adair, County, Dec.24th, 1869.[63]

---

[62] Ibid., C.L.R. James. pp. 12,13.
[63] The preceding 1-12 cases are included in "Report of Cases of Outrage, made in compliance with instructions of Major General Howard forwarding letter from War

Our ancestors were attacked and murdered so relentlessly that George Taylor was prompted to address the public and make them aware of the possible extermination of our ancestors. His letter is as follows:

"In the State of Alabama is found an organization known as the "Knights of the White Shield." The advertised object of this organization is to exterminate the Negro. Are we not forced then to organize for our own protection?

"It is not the purpose of this organization to injure or aid any political party, for the writer has never cast a ballot only for Republican candidates, except twice in local elections, when my judgment led me to vote the People's Party ticket, of which I am neither ashamed nor sorry.

"The time has come when the condition of our race in the south demands that every Negro in the north stand up to be counted with the race. We must strike at the root of the evil that threatens our existence and menaces our progress. We must hew to the line, let the chips fall where they may. Let us realize the fact that the welfare of our race and the lives of American citizens are paramount to the success of any political party. An enemy is an enemy and a friend is a friend, no matter what may be his political affiliation.

"We denounce state rights and adhere to the supremacy of the Federal government. We heartily endorse the Federal constitution, and are forever ready to offer our lives for its defense. Under it we claim the rights of citizenship and demand protection to our lives. We appeal to the lovers of liberty everywhere and the American people especially, in whom we still have faith, to assist us in peacefully securing what the law of the land, as well as the divine law of God already accord us: Equality before the law; protection to our lives.

"The National Colored Men's Protective Association of America will meet in national convention in the city of

---

Department, Adjutant Generals Office of January 23rd, 1867 requiring report of violations of "Civil Rights Bill" and action of Bureau officers."

Indianapolis, Ind., September 22d, 1892, for the purpose of furthering these ends.

"All friends of human liberty who sympathize with us in this effort for the protection of human life will be welcomed to our convention.

"Respectfully submitted to the public.   GEO. E. TAYLOR".[64]

THE KILLINGS CONTINUE
November 22, 1895
MADISONVILLE, Tex., Nov. 21-News has been received here of the lynching of a Negro in this part of Madison County on Tuesday night. He was accused of riding his horse over a little white girl and injuring her. On Wednesday it was discovered that the wrong Negro had been gotten hold of by the mob. The guilty one made his escape. (CHICAGO TRIBUNE)
MONROE, La., Oct. 22-Warren Eton, a negro, who made an insulting remark to a white woman Monday, was taken from the jail here early this morning by a mob and hanged to a nearby telegraph pole. Two masked men held up the jailer with pistols but other members of the mob made no attempt to conceal their identity.[65]
JOE NATHAN ROBERTS, 23 year-old war veteran, was shot and killed in Sardis, Georgia, when he failed to say "yes sir," to a white man in May of 1947. A student at Temple University, Philadelphia, on the GI Bill of Rights, Roberts was visiting relatives when he was killed. No one was tried for the murder.[66]

DESTRUCTION OF DISTRICTS AND TOWNS
Examples:
February 25. Five hundred National Guardsmen swarmed into the Negro section of Columbia, Tennessee, firing riot guns and

---

[64] Pres. *National Colored Men's Protective Ass'n of America.* Oskaloosa, Iowa, July 14, 1892.
[65] See: Ralph Ginsburgh, *100 Years of Lynching* (Baltimore 1988)
[66] William Patterson. *We Charge Genocide* (N.Y.1970) p.63

other firearms. Police opened up with machine guns on the Negroes barricaded in their homes. Every Negro business establishment in the two black business areas was completely wrecked.

The terror against the Negro community (Mink Slide) began officially the day before when MRS. GLADYS STEPHENSON and her son JAMES, a veteran had an argument with a radio repairman. The repairman kicked and slapped Mrs. Stephenson and tore the sleeves out of her coat. Her son, James Stephenson, came to her defense and was arrested immediately and beaten by the police. As a lynch mob formed on Court Square, friends spirited James Stephenson and his mother out of the state and the Negro community prepared to defend itself from attack and prevent any lynchings from occurring. A large number of Negroes were arrested and jailed.[67]

On the last day of May 1921 in Tulsa, Oklahoma, an African American named Rowland was accused of attacking a white elevator girl. The white community armed itself for the lynching. African Americans armed themselves to prevent a lynching. There was a confrontation between the lynch mob and the black community. The black community was able to hold the racist mob at bay until dawn the following day.

It was on the following day, when the alleged culprit had already been removed from the city, that major violence occurred. Armed whites participated in a mass assault upon the Negro section, most of which was burned during the rioting. Although heavy-armed resistance occasionally met the white attack, Negro activity was primarily defensive. Many fled the area and gave themselves up to white authorities. A Negro deputy sheriff was active in disarming many Negroes. What seems to have started as a result of the intention of some Negroes to prevent a possible lynching became, before its bloody conclusion, a massacre of Negroes reminiscent in

---

[67] Ibid., p.66.

character, if not in scale, of pogrom. Many people were killed, more Negroes than whites, and property damage in the Negro area amounted to almost total devastation of an area a mile square.[68]

One of the most famous cases known of the total destruction of African American towns is of the town of Rosewood on New Year's Day 1923. An unknown number of men and women were killed. One newspaper, the Miami Daily Metropolis, banner, was written as follows:

MANY DIE IN FLORIDA RACE WAR HUNDREDS OF WHITES BATTLE NEGROES AMBUSHED IN CABIN, FOUR WHITES, 20 BLACKS DEAD[69]

---

[68] Allen Grimshaw. *Racial Violence in the United States* (Chicago, IL. 1969) p.107.
[69] Michael D'orso, *Rosewood: Like Judgement Day* (N.Y. 1996) p.49.

SECTION II

Chapter 1

MARKS OF OPPRESSION

MENTAL HEALTH
Racism acts as a bulwark of resistance to prevent African Americans from making the achievements that the society encourages individuals to attempt. There is a lot of research evidence indicating this is a "critical psychological determinant" of mental disorder within the African American community. Drug addiction, alcoholism, homicides, dysfunctional families, inferiority complex, and a host of other problems are directly related to the impact of the dynamics of racism and oppression and how one reacts to it. Oppression impacts in such a way it brings out and nurtures the negative, self-defeating traits of the oppressed, throughout the world.

> The deterioration of mental health through a combination of poverty and persecution is not limited to Negro Americans. The Peruvian mestizo, barely managing to survive on the outskirts of Lima, presents a case in point. Mental illness, alcoholism, and family disorder are widespread, as well as the familiar personality syndrome of inferiority feelings, insecurity, and hostility. The human species

reacts to crushing oppression in much the same way the world over.[70]

We have not been an exception in our reactions to the tremendous oppression we have suffered under for the past 400 odd years. All oppressed people react emotionally the same way. We have demonstrated in our personalities, the devastation to our psyche caused by the institution of slavery. Most of the negative behavior we display can be traced directly back to slavery and how we were treated. Though we are moving progressively to rid ourselves of the negative legacy of slavery, we are still too heavily burdened with it.

The behavior of Africans was modified by the dynamics of slavery to the point they could be redefined as "negroes", "niggers", "samboes" and etc. These negative behavior reactions to slavery over a period of time became psychological traits. When stimulated by the oppressive social dynamics of neo-slavery these same traits expose themselves in our behavior today. Pavlov has demonstrated how the behavior (appetite) of white mice was modified (they began to salivate) in association of a dynamic (ringing bell) and that each following generation of mice would react much the same as its ancestors with only 33% of the stimulus (number of bell rings) needed for each preceding generation. It illustrated that by the fifth generation the stimulus needed (social dynamics) to uncover the same behavior was around 2% of the initial dynamics utilized to start the process of our negative behavior. Each time the stimulus (same social dynamics as slavery) is applied to us we are prompted to react a certain way through association of the dynamics and the required behavior. Just as Pavlov's experiment discloses, by the fifth generation the dynamic in its subtlest form will produce the desired negative results.

---

[70] Thomas Pettigrew, *A Profile of the Negro American* (Princeton 1964) p.80.

FEAR

Dr. Lerone Bennett refers to white power as being internalized by African Americans. He proposes it has been through the use of fear that the white nation was able to oppress and rule us for so many years. This is how nations have always controlled their subjects. What has occurred more or less is from the beginning; our able oppressors have shown us that they will kill us if we resist them. It has been our fear of death the oppressors have used as a handle to control us.

Kenneth Stampp, informs us on the method utilized by slave masters to produce the "perfect slave."

> Here, then, was the way to produce the perfect slave: accustom him to rigid discipline, demand from him unconditional submission, impress upon him his innate inferiority, develop in him a paralyzing fear of white men, train him to adopt the master's code of good behavior, and instill in him a sense of complete dependence.[71]

The Koreans during the 1940s and 50s used some of the methods the slavers used to instill fear in our ancestors. The following is an example from the lips of a slave informer of the master using the famous water pump torture to produce fear. They would tie the slave up securely about the water pump and direct a steady flow of water to his head and shoulders, and in a matter of time this flow of water would produce excruciating, unbearable pain.

> When the water first strikes the head and arms, it is not at all painful; but in a very short time, it produces the sensation that is felt when heavy blows are inflicted with large rods. This

---
[71] Kenneth M. Stampp. *Slavery*. (New York: 1963) p.148

> perception becomes more and more painful, until the skull bone and shoulder blades appear to be broken in pieces. Finally, all the faculties become oppressed; breathing becomes more and more difficult; until the eye-sight becomes dim, and animation ceases. This punishment is in fact a temporary murder; as all the pains are endured, that can be felt by a person who was deprived of life by being beaten with bludgeons.[72]

And they committed all manner of violence to infill our ancestors with fear. Because they feared the pain and an unknown death they tolerated being less than God created them to be. This internalized fear of white power made them feel insecure and inferior. This insecurity and inferiority plays out in our lives today as we interact with society and with each other.

ANGER

For hundreds of years we were chattel slaves. We have always resented our condition, but we have known that an open expression of violence would be brutally suppressed. Many of us learned to handle our hostilities in other ways, such as withdrawing and becoming angry and apathetic. Most of this anger we feel has been turned inward against ourselves. When anger becomes too much, we let it flow out, being very careful not to direct it towards the oppressor, but towards each other. Examples of this can be noted in drive-by shootings, homicides, and assaults we commit against our own people daily. Most of these acts are born out of frustration, stress, and hopelessness riding the crest of anger.

---

[72] Ball, Charles. *Slavery in the United States: A Narrative of the Life of Charles Ball, a Black Man Who Lived Forty Years in Maryland, South Carolina, and Georgia as a Slave.* New York: 1837, p.500.

ACHIEVEMENT

Slavery in most instances destroyed our ancestors' need to achieve. There was no incentive for their self-achievement. They were in a state of total dependency on the masters of the plantations. Vestiges of this dynamic have been continued down to today. Thomas Pettigrew provides his analysis of the reasons for low achievement among African Americans:

> Negroes in bondage, stripped of their African heritage, were placed in a completely dependent role. All of their rewards came not from independent initiative and enterprise, but from absolute obedience to a situation that severely depresses the need for achievement among all people.[73]

After emancipation many of our ancestors continued the behavior of dependency. I am sure there is a direct connection between our present state of dependency and our ancestors' dependent conditions during slavery.

PERSONAL DIGNITY

During the process of turning our ancestors from free people into "subservient slaves, the denial of personal dignity was also involved."[74] Now, when we encounter others and they observe us many see a race that is not to be taken or treated seriously. Black women are viewed as girls, mammies or permissive sexual objects. Black men are viewed as boys, shiftless, lazy, criminal, sex-crazed or any combination of the preceding. Because others view and treat us as such, we act accordingly. This whole process is evidently a continuing legacy of slavery.

In reducing us to servitude the oppressors took away our humanity, our self worth. In the process of witnessing our

---

[73] Thomas Pettigrew, *A Profile of the American Negro* (Princeton, NJ: 1964) p. 14.
[74] Ibid. P.99.

mothers, sisters, and daughters being raped and tortured without striking a blow for their protection many of us developed a sense of self-loathing or hatred for ourselves. Doctors William Greer and Price Cobbs, claim the institution of slavery still exist, in the minds and souls of all who were involved.

> The culture of slavery was never undone for either master or slave. The civilization that tolerated slavery dropped its slaveholding cloak but the inner feelings remained. The "peculiar institution" continues to exert its evil influence over the nation. The practice of slavery stopped over a hundred years ago, but the minds of our citizens have never been freed.[75]

HIGH BLOOD PRESSURE AND ETC.,

The process of and maintenance of slavery was very oppressive and it produced medical problems in our ancestors that still manifest themselves in our lives today as legacies. There are many negative behaviors and sicknesses in our midst. Most of them can be traced back to slavery.

> In particular, mental illness and hypertension appear in part to be direct outgrowths of racial discrimination, to be conspicuous 'marks of oppression'.[76]

Few medical problems are of more importance than high blood pressure, which leads to a myriad of other diseases. It promotes strokes, heart attacks, kidney failure, and a host of mortal and chronic sicknesses. It is known as the "silent killer."

---

[75] William H. Greer, Price M. Cobbs. *Black Rage* (p.26)
[76] Thomas Pettigrew. *A Profile of the Negro American* (Princeton 1964) p.99.

SECTION III

THE CRIMINALS

Chapter 1

THE U.S. GOVERNMENT

Slavery could not have reached the level it did in the United States without the consent of the government. The government often worked hand-in-hand with the slave owners. The government with its might and justice could have suppressed the trade at any time if it had chosen to do so. The government as a matter of fact did the opposite by making slavery a lawful institution and sanctioning and regulating the exploitation of our ancestors' labor. Some white American citizens were against the institution of slavery but many others and their government were for it. The government was more interested in preparing for and suppressing slave revolts than suppressing slavery.

Constitutional scholar Mary Frances Berry informs us of the following:

> In the Second Congress, a bill was passed on May 2, 1792, which provided that the state militias could be called out to execute the laws of the Union, **suppress**[*] insurrections, and repel invasions.[77]

---

[*] My emphasis
[77] Mary Frances Berry. *Black Resistance, White Law* (N.Y. 1971) p.8.

The Federal government moved to prepare for any uprisings from our ancestors that threatened the security of the slave system. Congress even demanded in its treaties with the Indians that they return escaped slaves back to their masters.

> One of the first treaties made by President Washington supported the claims of Georgia slaveholders. The August 7, 1790, treaty with the Creek Indians in Georgia reasserted the demands made in the earlier treaties: the Creeks were bound to return black fugitives to their masters, even if these fugitives were living in Florida among the Seminoles.[78]

U.S. GOVERNMENT SANCTIONED TERRORISTS

From the beginning the United States government passed laws that were detrimental to our oppressed ancestors, but provided legal recognition for racist terrorist. The crime of the U.S.A., and State governments in connection with the paramilitary, terrorist groups that spread terror and death through out our captive nation (African American), was in the act of providing legal and corporate status for them. The following is a partial list of the most well known ones the United States government and its agencies legitimized:

1. Original Southern Klans, Inc. (Georgia)
2. Knights of the Ku Klux Klan of Florida, Inc.
3. Federated Klans of Alabama, Inc.
4. Knights of the Kavaliers, Inc. (Virginia)
5. United Sons of Dixie, Inc. (Tennessee)
6. American Shores Patrol, Inc. (Virginia)
7. American Keystone Society, Inc. (Pennsylvania)

---

[78] Ibid., p. 31.

8. The Christian American, Inc. (Texas)
9. The Fact Finders, Inc. (Georgia)
10. Fight for Free Enterprise, Inc. (Texas)
11. Free White Americans, Inc. (Tennessee)
12. Mason-Dixon Society, Inc. (Kentucky)
13. We, the People, Inc. (Georgia)
14. Vigilantes, Inc. (Georgia)
15. Veterans & Patriots Federation of Labor, Inc. (Tenn.)
16. Order of American Patriots, Inc. (Texas)
17. Southern Committee to Uphold the Constitution, Inc. (Texas)
18. The Patrick Henrys, Inc. (Georgia)
19. Southern States Industrial Council, Inc. (Tenn.)
20. National Small Businessmen's Assoc. Inc. (Mich)"[79]

TUSKEGEE/SYPHILIS EXPERIMENT

In 1932, the USPHS, allegedly interested in studying untreated tertiary (final stage) syphilis, selected an experimental group consisting of 400 poor, uneducated African American males from Tuskegee, Alabama, to serve as study subjects (guinea pigs). The men were never told about their life threatening disease, and worse, there was a conspiracy that denied them treatment. Another 200 healthy black men served as control subjects. Both groups were carefully and objectively observed for decades.

According to James H. Jones, author of Bad Blood, in 37 years up to 25% of the men in the experiment died from syphilis related diseases.

> ... as of 1969, at least 28 and perhaps as many as 100 men had died as a direct result of complications caused by syphilis. Others had

---
[79] William Patterson, Ed. We *Charge Genocide*. (N.Y. 1951) p.158.

> developed syphilis-related heart conditions that may have contributed to their deaths."[80]

Other victims included the untreated wives of the victims, many of them also became infected, and some of their children may have been born with birth defects.

These officials of the PHP utilized the dangerous and dreaded "spinal tap" procedure on these unaware victims to withdraw fluids for testing for paresis. The side effects of this procedure included, "severe headaches that may last for days or even weeks are common as the numbness or stiffness (partial) in the neck or limbs."[81] The officials decided to deceive the victims and get the procedures done to as many as possible before they suffered its aftereffects and word spread about them. Here is what the Public Health Official, Dr. Raymond A. Vonderlehr wrote:

> My idea in bringing them in large groups is to get the procedure completed in a given area before the negro population has been able to find out just what is going on. Individual patients would be told that they are coming in for an examination but they would remain all night after we had them here, and the details of the puncture techniques should also be kept from them as far as possible.[82]

One of the reasons given by Dr. John R Heller years later for refusing the men treatment for this induced disease was, "the men's status did not warrant ethical debate. They were subjects, not patients; clinical material, not sick people."[83]

---

[80] J H Jones. *Bad Blood*. New York: 1981,P.2
[81] ibid., p. 123.
[82] Vonderlehr to Clark, January 12, 1933, NA-WNRC
[83] Quoted in, *Bad Blood*. P.179.

The Public Health department has already confessed to this crime against the black family and the black man in particular. We must guard against this ever happening again.

BIO/CHEMICAL EXPERIMENT IN GUYANA?

It has been reported that many of lethal drugs used to facilitate the death of nearly 1,000 people in Jonestown, were the same drugs the CIA was developing for mind control. Independent investigators have documented many connections between the CIA and Peoples Temple.

> The Guyanese Chief Medical Examiner testified in court that 80 percent of the bodies he examined showed signs of forcible injections. Jim Jones, the self-proclaimed leader of the "People's Temple" which moved to Guyana from San Francisco, and one of his aides, had CIA connections. The father of Jonestown leader Larry Layton was head of CBW Research at the Army's Dugway Proving Grounds in the 1950s. The elder Layton admitted contributing $25,000 to the People's Temple. According to Judge, "Public exposure [in the mid-1970s] of experiments in U.S. prisons and mental institutions was, in all likelihood, a major impetus for relocating this testing to the jungles of a virtually unknown country."[84]

The one thing that struck me as odd was the orderly way the bodies of all 900 of these people were arranged. Its as though the "cool aid" somehow forced each person to lie one besides the other, with all their heads pointing in the same direction. The effects of disorder one expected during a mass poisoning

---

[84] R. Lederer, Precedents for Aids? Chemical-biological warfare, medical experiments, and population control. Covert Action Information bulletin 1987; 28:33-42.

was not depicted, but rather a macabre orderliness prevailed. One would suppose by the visual presentation of the many bodies, that someone besides them was responsible for laying the bodies in that fashion.

Perhaps you may think this is a bit paranoid. But, I refer you to the Tuskegee experiment, the mind control experiments in Vacaville, California prison, and perhaps many hundreds more, and dare your logical mind to say the implications are far fetched. The worst you can say against the implication, is that because a fellow African American makes it, it is a "healthy paranoia." We are in desperate need of mental and physical overhauling. It will take a massive effort to correct these intentionally inflicted diseases. All who caused the wear and tear on our minds and brokenness of our bodies, including those who have profited from the same, should take responsibility for returning what was stolen and repairing what was broken.

THE CONSTITUTION

The constitution under careful analysis will disclose a document that is pro-slavery and anti-African American. The African American was considered as mere property by its framers and consequently had no rights or protection in its proclamations. As a matter of fact, it guaranteed the slavers their right to enslavement of our ancestors (their property) for an extended period of time, to 1808. The Supreme Court under Judge Taney decided that African Americans in relation to the people (white citizens),

> ...yet remained subject to their authority, and had no rights or privileges but such as those who held the power and the government might chose to grant them.[85]

---
[85] Boller. *A More Perfect Union* .vol.1. (Boston 1988) p. 189.

Judge Taney claims there are two clauses in the constitution that indicate the African Americans were considered as distinct from "the people" or "citizens" of the government that existed at the time of the framing of the constitution.

> One of these clauses reserves to each of the thirteen states the right to import slaves until the year 1808.[86]

The logic being that if they had been provided rights and protection under the constitution, slavery would have been completely outlawed by the constitution's very being, which was not the case. The other clause maintained the

> Right of property of the master, by delivering up to him any slave who may have escaped from his service, and be found within their respective territories. And these provisions show, conclusively, that neither the description of persons therein referred to, nor their descendants, were embraced in any of the other provisions of the constitution; for certainly these two clauses were not intended to confer on them or their posterity the blessings of liberty, or any of the personal rights so carefully provided for citizen.[87]

When we reflect on this opinion of the highest court of the land, we must admit, either of its truth, or the belief in its truthfulness by "the people" and their governmental and societal institutions. They excluded African-Americans because we still have not been accorded the rights and privileges of "the people" granted by the constitution. One of the main grounds on which the court

---

[86] Ibid., p. 191.
[87] Ibid., 191.

ruled against Dred Scott was that as an African he could not be a citizen of the United States and therefore had no rights to sue in a Federal court.

If we (African Americans) had been included in the phrase "of the people", or even remotely considered as an integral part of the political entity (USA) created by the constitution, there would be no need for Amendments to the constitution or Affirmative Action programs or Civil Rights bills. These various bills and amendments are merely patches added to breaches in the original constitutional document. Jesus Christ clearly teaches:

> No man putteth a piece of new cloth unto an old garment for that which is put in to fill it up taketh from the garment, and the rent is made worse.[88]

The various bills and amendments attached to the guarantees of the constitution for the benefit of African Americans have done just that. Hasn't the country been in turmoil over affirmative action programs? Wasn't there a small-scale battle concerning the civil rights bill? No other ethnic group or race in the U.S.A. needs additions to the constitution to be accorded the rights of citizens. Why is it that we (African Americans) need special legislation and programs for our protection? Is it because we are not really considered as part of the political entity (U.S.A.) created by the constitution for "we the people?"

Jesus Christ offers a solution in his teachings for the above situation.

> Neither do men put new wine into old bottles: else the bottles break, and the wine runneth out,

---
[88] *Matthhew* 9:15.

and the new bottle perish: but they put new wine into new bottles, and both are preserved.[89]

It appears as though Jesus anticipated our condition and the attempts by human frailty to fill old wineskins (constitution) with new wine (equal rights) for our people. He teaches that the wineskins will perish, that the correct way is to secure new wineskins. Perhaps we need to push for a new constitution that includes all the people in the U.S.A.

MODERN PRISON SYSTEMS

It has been claimed by various authorities that over one-third of African American males between the ages of 18 to 35 are either in or associated with the penal system. Well over 50% of all prison inmates are African Americans. Something is wrong with this system especially since African Americans are only 12% of the population. The prison system is nothing more for African American males than an extension of the slave plantation.

The prison system has its slave drivers (guards, etc.). It exploits the labor and dignity of prisoners. There appears to be three functions to the prison system: 1. Remove certain people out of society, 2. Revenge, and, 3. Economic exploitation. By 1991 this industry was $37 billion and growing.[90] There is a continuity of historical flow from the prison system back through the chain gangs (free labor) to the plantations.

COURTS OF JUSTICE

John Henderson Affair:

CORSICANA, Tex., Mar. 13 - John Henderson, the negro accused of murdering Mrs. Younger, was burned at the stake by a mob of 5,000 persons in this city today. He purportedly had

---

[89] *Matthew* 9:17.
[90] Clarence J. Munford. *Race And Reparations* (Trenton, N.J. 1996) p.325.

confessed his guilt. Subsequently the coroner held an inquest over his remains and the jury returned a verdict commending the mob for its act of horror.[91]

Rodney King Affair:

George Holiday videotaped several policemen beating Rodney King unmercifully and savagely. A Los Angeles Grand Jury indicted Sgt. Stacey Koon, Laurence M. Powell, Theodore J. Briseno, and Timothy E. Wind for the uncalled for and inhuman beating of King. A jury consisting of ten whites, one Hispanic and one Asian acquitted these policemen on April 29, 1992.

Amadou Diallo Overkill:

All of the police officers have been acquitted after firing 41 shots at an unarmed African male and mortally wounding him with 19 of those shots. Some of the bullets entered from the bottom of his feet. However, white power through its court of justice has freed these badge-wearing murderers. Were you really surprised by the verdict?

I am sure neither of the previous examples surprised most African Americans. We understand that is the way the game is played and we are not players but the played. The game usually ends the same way except on very rare occasions.

POLICE TERROR

There has been a continuous attack by police departments on the African American communities and individuals since their origin as patrollers during slavery to the present. The patrollers originated as a "custom to please a few slaveholders and to help them control their stock."[92]

---

[91] See: Ralph Ginsburg's *100 Years of Lynchings*.
[92] Bruce, Henry Clay. *The New Man: Twenty-Nine Years A Slave, Twenty-Nine Years a Free Man*. Recollections of H.C. Bruce. N.Y.: 1895, p.96.

One slave reported the following consequence for being found by a patroller without a pass.

> Got to have paper. Got to carry you paper. Dem patrollers put you cross a log! Beat you to death.[93]

They were often armed and some even rode horses accompanied by attack dogs. They had the right to assault any slave who was caught where they shouldn't be without a pass. Many times they killed slaves who tried to escape their questions. Some hired themselves out to widows and other female slave owners to whip their slaves for fifty cents apiece.

Lewis Clark left the following eyewitness account of the cruelty of these patrollers.

> [The] greatest scoundrel is always captain of the band of patrols. They are the off-scouring of all things; the refuse, the fag end, the ears and tails of slavery; the scales and fins of fish; the tooth and tongues of serpents. They are the very fool's cap of baboons, the echo of parrots, the wallet and satchel of polecats, the scum of stagnant pool, the exuvial, the worn-out skins of slaveholders. They are, emphatically, the servants of servants, and slaves of the devil; they are the meanest, and lowest and worst of all creation. Like starved wharf rats, they are out nights, creeping into slave cabins to see if they have an old bone there; drive out husbands from their own beds, and then take their places. They get up all sorts of pretences, false as their lying tongues can make them, and

---

[93] Quoted in Charles Joyner. *Down By The Riverside*. Chicago:1985, p.132.

then whip the slaves and carry a gory lash to the master, for a piece of bread.[94]

They whipped us, killed us, raped our women, and most importantly, they controlled us for the slave owner's benefit. The modern policemen have their origins in that madness.

THE INFAMOUS NEW ORLEANS RIOT OF 1866
In a letter from General Sheridan to General Grant:

> IT WAS NOT A RIOT. IT WAS AN ABSOLUTE MASSACRE BY THE POLICE, WHICH WAS NOT EXCELLED IN MURDEROUS CRUELTY BY THAT OF FORT PILLOW. IT WAS A MURDER WHICH THE MAYOR AND POLICE OF THE CITY PERPETRATED WITHOUT THE SHADOW OF NECESSITY... FURTHERMORE, I BELIEVE IT WAS PREMEDITATED.

This General of the U.S. army claims the police carried out a planned paramilitary attack against the freedmen within the first year of their supposed release from slavery. This should be accepted as fact because it comes from a reliable source. The following telegram was received, July 31, 1866, from New Orleans, LA. It is the statement of another reliable witness.

Major Gen. O.O. HOWARD:

> The riot has been suppressed. I have declared marital law in the city. About 40 persons have

---

[94] Lewis Clarke. *Narratives of the Sufferings of Lewis Clarke During a Captivity of More Than Twenty-Five Years Among the Algerines of Kentucky.* Boston: 1845, p.114.

been killed and a large number wounded nearly all being friendly to the Convention.

A. Baird
Major General.
Office United States Military Telegraph,
Headquarters. War Department

GEORGE WADDELL was shot in the back and slain in his Brooklyn, New York home by Brooklyn police on February 18, 1949. Police entered his home without a warrant and with no offense charged against Waddell. They claimed they were looking for a gambling game when they forced entry into Waddell's home. No evidence of gambling was found.[95]

February 5, 1945. - A policeman of Freeport, L.I., New York, shot and killed PFC. CHARLES FERGUSON and his brother, ALFONSO FERGUSON. A third brother, SEAMAN THIRD CLASS JOSEPH FERGUSON was wounded in the shoulder and thrown into the brig, while a fourth brother, RICHARD FERGUSON, was arrested and sentenced to 100 days in jail. The brothers had protested Jim-crow at a local cafe, where the proprietor had refused them service because they were Negroes. After the killings, Freeport police threw a cordon around the bus terminal and stationed men with Tommy guns and tear gas there, saying that they wanted to "prevent a possible uprising of local Negroes." Investigation proved that none of the brothers were armed, they were peaceably on their way from the cafe to the bus station when the policeman attacked them. Witnesses, including two white women, made affidavits that the brothers were not disorderly. The killer-policeman was exonerated by the Chief of Police and by the Nassau Grand Jury. An investigation ordered by Governor Dewey after five months of

---

[95] Patterson ed. *We Charge Genocide* (New York 1970) p.11.

organized protest, whitewashed the police, the grand jury that refused to indict the policeman, and the District Attorney of Nassau County. The investigation also denied the lawyer for the slain brothers' families the right to cross examination and the right to put specific questions to witnesses.[96]

1971 War Attack Against Blacks by Law Enforcement

Imari Bubakari Obadele has left the following recording of attacks against his government[*] by Federal and City police military squads.

> Much is made of the fact that when a small army of FBI agents and City Policemen attacked the RNA Government Residence in Jackson (Mississippi) at dawn on August 18, 1971, one policeman was killed and an FBI agent and a policeman were wounded. Little is said about the fact that the police and FBI claimed to be seeking a man on an FBI flight warrant - whose location they were *not* certain of (they sent officers to two locations simultaneously) and who was not found either at the Lewis Street house or the Lynch Street office. According to their own sworn testimony, the FBI and police fired gas guns (which sound like shotguns) into the house 75 second after they arrived and before they had any sign of resistance from inside. Indeed, FBI Agent Lester Amman testified that he fired first and that he fired gas cannisters into the *bedroom* of Interior Minister Offogga Qudduss (sn Wayne James of Camden, N.J.), 23, and his three-months pregnant

---

[96] Ibid.

[*] The second president of the provisional government of the Republic of New Africa.

wife, Njeri (sn Toni Renee Austin). Both were in bed.[97]

The Police (Federal and local) are the most crucial institutions of the white oppressor nation in maintaining the colonial status of the African American people. It is through their patrolling that they keep us oppressed in the ghettoes. They accomplish this by harassing us without provocation when we are found outside of our assigned areas (ghettoes, the new plantations). They shoot and kill us at the slightest provocation or their imagination. Consequently, if we are to overcome our oppressive colonization we must inevitably confront and deal with the police departments (the local armies of the oppressors). Small teams (lynch mobs or policemen) of the oppressors' terrorist army lynched over 5,000 African Americans from 1860 - 1960.[98]

We have been kidnapped, raped, tortured, dismembered, our labor has been stolen, and we are still victims of racism. There are laws on the international level that prohibit such savage oppressive treatment.[*]

---

[97] Imari Abubakari Obadele. *Foundations of the Black Nation*. p.109.
[98] Ralph Ginsburg. *100 Years of Lynchings*. (Baltimore, MD. 1988)
[*] See appendix

Chapter 2

ROLE OF RELIGIOUS INSTITUTIONS AND OTHER GROUPS

Catholic Church Involvement

In 1441 Captain Goncalves made an attack on the west coast of Africa, captured ten Africans and took them back to Prince Henry (called the Navigator). The prince was pleased with the capture and sought an audience with the pope who was always pleased with the spread of Christianity. The pope was advised that Henry intended to attack Africa and make a conquest. The pope (Nicholas V) promised he would grant forgiveness to all that participated in the war if the infidels were brought into the Christian fold.

Pope Nicholas V issued a papal bull in 1455 authorizing Portugal to reduce all infidel people to servitude. According to Robert E. Hood in his book *Begrimed and Black*,

> His 1454 bull *Dum diversa* authorized and sanctioned the invasion of Africa by the Portuguese, permitting them to invade, search out, capture, conquer, and subjugate all Saracens and pagans whatsoever and other enemies of Christ wherever they exist...in those and adjoining regions and in the further and more remote areas.[99]

---

[99] Robert E. Hood. *Begrimed And Black: Christian Traditions on Blacks and Blackness.* (MN. 1994) p.117.

In 1492 Columbus "discovered" the new world and set in motion the scramble of European countries to expand. Two European powers, Spain and Portugal, in their quest for riches sought and found an arbitrator to prevent conflict between them with the pope, in the competition to exploit Africa.

In 1493 the pope of the Catholic Church issued several Papal bulls granting the Portuguese the right to search out and exploit the East and Spain the West. The war against our people escalated.

Robert E. Hood advises us that the very first official shipment of Africans to the Americas was "escorted by Catholic priests".[100]

The Church, in general, supported the slave trade and in return the trade supported the church. Eric Williams claims at least three divisions of the Catholic Church were not only supporting but also profiteering slavers.

> The Spaniards saw in it an opportunity of converting the heathen, and the Jesuits, Dominicans and Franciscans were heavily involved in sugar cultivation which meant slave holding.[101]

The Church was heavily involved in this scandalous profit-making venture. This involvement did not recently start, but has its genesis in the 15th century at the beginning of the exploitative slave trade. The church was morally hypocritical then, just as many of its congregations are today.

William Stringfellow bears witnesses to the Church's hypocrisy in her professed morality and involvement in the enslavement and oppression of our people.

---

[100] Ibid. p.115.
[101] Eric Williams. Capitalism and Slavery (N.Y. 1966) p. 42.

> ...the white ecclesiastical institutions in America are and have long been directly implicated in profiteering from slavery, segregation and other forms of white supremacy through the investment and management of their endowments and other holdings in the American economy. The predominant social witness of the churches racially, for generations, has been incarnated in the wealth and property of white religion, and not in the redundant preaching or pronouncements about racial justice. Indeed, such utterances made in the context of white racism institutionalized in church economics can only be construed as gratuitous hypocrisy. The wonder of it all is how a people can so deceive themselves, perhaps they only can when the deception is practiced in the name of God.[102]

The Church was both anti and pro-slavery. However, the Church was both immoral and hypocritical to give sanctions to the enslavement of human beings. The very Christ, whom the Church holds up, proclaimed He came to the world to "preach deliverance to the captives."[103] Many additional nails must have been driven into the Lord's body by the Church's participation in the horrific and exploitative oppression of our people. History has pulled the covers off the Church's real morality and left her exposed in her naked harlotries.

The Christian Reformation

Careful analysis of the teachings of Calvin and Luther will reveal a theology that encouraged the perpetuation of slavery. We need to understand the role slavery played in the

---

[102] William Stringfellow. *Reparations: Repentance as a Necessity. The Black Manifesto* (N.Y. 1969) p.57.
[103] *Luke* 4:18.

development of capitalism, combined with the greed that is inherent with the profit motive and Martin Luther and John Calvin's teachings that helped accelerate the rise of the capitalist spirit.

Luther may have denounced bankers but he avidly preached religious individualism and that charging usury (interest) was okay.

> ...He preached a religious individualism that was bound to weaken the hold of all churches on men's minds, and was certain to carry over into economic life. When the officials of the city on Danzig asked Luther whether they should put down usury, he replied that the taking of usury should be left to each man's conscience.[104]

Calvin believed interest on loans was proper as long as it was not too excessive and was legal.

> In general, Calvin felt that credit, profits, and interest were a normal part of business and were not to be condemned unless they were excessive. Furthermore he and his followers preached a way that was exactly in line with the needs and ideas of growing capitalism.[105]

Calvin's position on interest prompted Max Weber to remark that Calvin's "teaching made it possible to worship God and Mammon at the same time." Many other scholars have pointed out that it was in lands that practiced Calvinism-- essentially Holland, England and France, where capitalism grew rapidly. Lest we forget, slavery gave rise to this capitalism.

---

[104] Shepard Bancroft Clough and Charles Woolsey Cole. *Economic History of Europe*. Boston, 1952, p.152
[105] Ibid. pp.152,153.

The Church through its Reformation leaders such as Luther and Calvin backed the profit scheme in interest charges, which is a foundation pillar of capitalism. One fact we can agree on is that the rise of capitalism was connected to slavery and the Reformation period.

Jewish Involvement

Jews were involved in the Atlantic slave trade since it's beginning. They were agents, navigators, ship owners, insurers, investors, slavers, plantation owners, and etc. When the ships crossed the seas with our wretched ancestors chained in the holds, Jews were among the ship owners and transporters, and profiteers in the flesh of our captured ancestors.

> They came with ships carrying African blacks to be sold as slaves. The traffic in slaves was a royal monopoly, and the Jews were often appointed as agents for the Crown in their sale. When the king granted Pedro Gomez Reinal the exclusive right to import slaves into the colonies, the contract contained a clause permitting Gomez to have on his ship two Portuguese who would be in charge of the sale of the Negroes and do anything else necessary among the people of the sea.[106]

After 1790, Jews controlled the slave trade in the state of Rhode Island. Brothers with the family name of De Wolf were at the helm of this control.[107] There were many other Jewish slave barons involved in this business. Two of the most notoriously successful ones were partners, Aaron Lopez and Jacob Rodriguez Rivera. Aaron owned approximately thirty

---

[106] Liebman, *New World Jewry.* p.170.
[107] James Pope – Hennessy. *A Study of the Atlantic Slave Traders: 1441-1807* (N.Y. 1967) p.239.

ships.[108] These persons were members of God's "chosen people" who supposedly had been the objects of oppression all their lives, now involved in the horrendous oppression of our ancestors. John Pope-Hennessy answers the question that begs to be answered in this peculiar situation.

> Like the Jewish slavers of Jamaica, Lopez and his ramified relatives were of Sephardic origin. Persecuted in Portugal, these families had sought sanctuary in America, where they could practice their faith in freedom and grow rich respectably. You might have supposed, might not, that a national and religious group, which had chosen freedom, would hesitate at making a fortune by enslaving others? You would have been sadly wrong.[109]

The cold facts are that Jews did so much slaving from Rhode Island that it became the new center of the slave trade. Rhode Island became the "Liverpool" of America. Jews made their venture in slaving very profitable. To speak of "Jewish" involvement is too general. Lets put a face on some of the Jewish slavers. The following is a sampling of some real Jewish dealers, owners, investors and shippers operating from the 'Big Apple.'[*]

> "Issack Asher, Jacob Barsimson, Joseph Bueno, Solomon Myers Cohen, Jacob Fonseca , Aberham Franckfort, Jacob Franks, Daniel Gomez, David Gomez, Isaac Gomez, Lewis Gomez , Mordecai Gomez, Rebekah Gomez, Ephraim Hart, Judah Hays, Harmon Hendricks, Uriah Hendricks, Uriah

---

[108] Ibid., p.241.
[109] Ibid., p. 241.
[*] New York City.

> Hyam, Abraham Isaacs, Joshua Isaacs, Samuel Jacobs, Benjamin S. Judah, Cary Judah, Elizabeth Judah, Arthur Levy, Eleazar Levy, Hayman Levy, Isaac H. Levy, Jacob Levy, Joseph Israel Levy, Joshua Levy, Moses Levy, Uriah Phillips Levy, Isaac R. Marques, Moses Michaels, Manuel Myers, Seixas Nathan, Simon Nathan, Rodrigo Pacheco, David Pardo, Isaac Pinheiro, Rachel Pinto, Morris Jacob Raphall, Abraham Sarzedas, Moses Seixas, Solomon Simpson, Nathan Simson, Simja De Torres, Benjamin Wolf, Alexander Zuntz."[110]

Jews were not just incidental or peripheral to the Atlantic slave trade. But were major players in the trade in black flesh. They ate from the same trough as the other slavers in the country. They were just like everybody else.

> Jews were indistinguishable from other White Americans in their attitudes and treatment of Blacks. When "King Cotton" dominated the South, Jews began to enter the planter class in substantial numbers. Slave-dealing was an extremely profitable business particularly in the lower South which required a constant resupply for its newly developed plantations. The upper South produced more slaves through natural increase and breeding than its over-worked soil required creating interregional commercial opportunities. Plantation supply became the bread and butter Jewish enterprise with their goods of all

---

[110] *The Nation of Islam. The Secret Relationship Between Blacks and Jews.* (Boston, MS:1993) p.97.

descriptions keeping the Southern slave economy in motion.[111]

They treated their chattel property no different than the other slave masters. It didn't matter that their traditions spoke about how God had delivered them from Pharaoh's oppression, now, they were in the role of slave masters. Joseph Weinberg shares the following with us about the reality of the Jewish slaver.

> In their treatment and dealings with slaves Jews behaved no better and no worse than other white men; at times they beat recalcitrant slaves and had their share of black runaways.[112]

They made profits, and neither the moral issue about slavery, or their own history of oppression by others fazed them. The slave system rewarded them profitably and consequently they defended the system.

> "For the most part they had acquired wealth and owned numerous slaves whom they exploited for the development of their resources. Their prosperity and long tenancy had won them prestige equal to that of the non-Jewish natives, and they were not only completely at home amid their surroundings, but, naturally, supported and sanctioned the institutions that had been so propitious to them, providing them with wealth, position and comfort. Like other wealthy Southern land and slave owners they were convinced that their financial stability depended upon maintaining the services of the negro slaves. It is, therefore, hardly surprising that they became

---
[111] ibid., p.121.
[112] Joseph Weinberg, p.34

staunch upholders of the slavery system, in their unwillingness to relinquish these personal benefits.[113]

The charge of Jewish participation in the Atlantic slave trade, and a sea of historical facts supports their realizing huge profits from the sale, and dehumanization of our ancestors. Consequently, when we present the final bill for the losses and damages that others have caused us to suffer, Jews must be among those expected to do everything possible to right the wrong that was/is done to us.

We now approach at a dazzling speed the final showdown rising on the horizon. Every battle we have waged against the enemy since prehistoric times to Egypt through Mali, Songhai, Ghana, Harlem, Detroit, and Watts were dress rehearsals for the upcoming final confrontation. This will be the battle that will end the war. The battle that Nat Turner prophesied about, when hieroglyphic words will appear on the leaves in the fields, and blood drops shall cover the kernels of corn, will be upon us. Black spirits and white spirits will be engaged in battle. It will be the final confrontation. We can face it confidently knowing that we are on the side that will be victorious, the side of righteousness, the side of the oppressed, the side of the returning cosmic liberator, Jesus Christ.

American Indian Involvement

It is true that some Indian tribes did fight side by side with African Americans during the Seminole wars in Florida against the common enemy, the white slave master and his supporters. It is also true that the major tribes were as involved in slaving as Thomas Jefferson, or the southern plantation slave owner.

In the early colonial period in America, Europeans took great care in discouraging alliances between our ancestors and

---

[113] G. Cohen, pp.84-85. Page 120. *Secret Relationship*

Indians in most of the Indian treaties. Many of these treaties required Indians to aid in the capture of runaway slaves and to turn them over to local authority or owners.

Indians were involved in slave trading and early on found how it extremely profitable it was. By the end of the 18th century, some Indian tribes were slave traders and owners, and fought alongside the Southern Confederacy in the Civil War to maintain slavery and protect their economic interests.

1. In 1824, there were 1,277 black slaves being held among 15,560 Cherokees.
2. In 1861, 25,000 Choctaw and Chickasaw Indians owned more than 5,000 black slaves.
3. In a treaty at Fort Smith, Arkansas, in September 1865, the Choctaws and Chickasaws were paid $300,000 by the U.S. government for a district of lands west of the 98-degree longitude. Essentially, the treaty provided that the U.S. government pay the Choctaw and Chickasaw Legislatures $300,000 plus 5% interest for the land contingent upon the Indians drafting laws and rules to free all their black slaves, and give "each black slave and their descendants, 40 acres of land from each nation.
4. Also, in addition to the 80 acres to have been given to each slave, each tribe was to give each slave "$1.00 per capita" The treaty further stipulated that should the Indian legislatures not craft these laws for black slaves within a two-year time period from the ratification of the treaty, the $300,000 shall cease to be held in trust for the Indians and given instead to the black ex-slaves.
5. A contingency of ex-slaves traveled to Washington, D.C in the early 1870s and complained to Congress that they never received the 80 acres of land nor the monies.

These Indian tribes owe our ancestors a very large debt.

SECTION IV

Chapter 1

MODERN EXAMPLES OF REPARATION PAYMENTS

JEWS

Many historical books, television documentaries, and movies have disclosed to the world the satanic holocaust in which over 6,000,000 Jews were murdered in Europe. Their wealth was stolen and they were uprooted and transported to various locales to be systematically put to death. As a result the survivors of the horror and their descendents suffered many physical and psychological problems.

In 1952 the Federal Republic of Germany came to an agreement with Israel for the payment of $822 million, following a claim to Israel, which was limited to the costs of resettling 500,000 Jews who had migrated from Nazi controlled countries. In 1990 Austria paid $25 million to survivors of the holocaust.

JAPANESE

As recently as 12 years ago, in 1990, the U.S.A. government paid Japanese Americans $1.2 billion, for their forced internment on the west coast during the Second World War. The professed reason for the forced internment was for national defense, because the United States was engaged in war with Japan.

> During 1942-46, some 77,000 American citizens of Japanese ancestry and 43,000 Japanese nationals, most of whom were permanent U.S. residents, were summarily deprived of liberty and property without criminal charges, and without trial of any kind. Several persons were also violently deprived of life. All persons of Japanese ancestry on the West Coast were expelled from their homes and confined in inland detention camps. The sole basis of these actions was ancestry -citizenship, age; loyalty or innocence of wrongdoing did not matter. Japanese-Americans were the only ones singled out for mass incarceration. German and Italian nationals and American citizens of German and Italian ancestries were not imprisoned en masse.[114]

It was wrong to force the Japanese people to live in the relocation centers during the Second World War and it was just to pay reparations to them. However, the conditions of the relocation centers did not compare to the hell the Jews experienced in the Nazi concentration camps in Europe during the Second World War. Neither the conditions of the Japanese nor Jews compare to the conditions the African Americans have survived during their forced migration in the holds of those horrible slave ships or, on many plantations in the south and other places. This is not a "we suffered more than you" diatribe but is merely a humble attempt to point out that if one wronged group deserves it we all do.

---

[114] A Pamphlet by the Japanese Redress Organization.

The following is a report on the general situation of the Japanese in those camps. Some, we are to understand had jobs and,

> ...left the camps for employment outside. Those who remained in the centers until the end of the war did so primarily because they preferred the security and comfort of the camps to the uncertainties of life on the outside.
> Although the relocation centers were established under the difficult circumstances of the early wartime months, the authorities made every effort to minimize the hardship for re-locaters. The camps were self-governing and people who worked received compensation.[115]

The preceding quotation is not used to imply that the Japanese did not deserve reparations. Instead it is meant to show that if the Japanese deserved reparation, African Americans most surely deserve it. The payments to each Japanese person averaged $20,000.

The U.S.A. also paid the following reparations in 1971, $1 billion and 44 million acres of land to Alaska natives, $81 million to the Klamaths of Oregon, $105 million, in 1985 to the Sioux of South Dakota, $12.3 million to the Seminoles of Florida, $31 million to the Chippewas of Wisconsin, and $32 million to the Ottawas of Michigan in 1986.

REPARATIONS PAID TO OTHERS:
Japan paid to South Korea for acts committed during the Japanese occupation of Korea.
Iraq paid for its invasion of Kuwait.
Canada paid $230 million to the Japanese in 1988.

---

[111] Baker, Lillian. The *Japanning of America* (Medford 1991) p.44.

Canada paid 250,000 square miles of land to Indians and Eskimos.
America paid reparations to Germany 1919-33
Florida paid to the survivors of the infamous Rosewood holocaust.[116]

    The Rosewood affair is the first recording of the United States Government in modern times paying reparations on a claim filed by African Americans. In this action the precedent for reparation to African Americans has been set. We at least know that the payment of our future claims for African people for our stolen labor and the holocaust that we experienced is within the realm of possibilities. Our task is to delve into that realm and make that possibility a reality. We must first educate our people and create an international mass African peoples' movement whose goal is the attainment of reparations for all African people by any means necessary. We must then present our just case before the world court for a judgment on the matter. If justice is curtailed in this highest court in the world we must be willing to take it to the next level, then the next until justice and freedom are ours. We must not be motivated by revenge but justice. Justice is a high moral concept while revenge is low and immoral. It really places you on the same moral level with the oppressor. To be revengeful is to operate from a base of hate. We must always operate from a base of love. That is love of God, love of freedom, love of others and love of self.

    Maybe we need to understand that when we operate from a fear of God reference we will protect God's Holy Temple (our bodies) from being desecrated by any abomination. This means if God is in you, then you are one of His lights in the world and you must prevent any and everything from extinguishing that

---

[116] January, 1923 destruction of African American town of Rosewood, Florida and massacre that took the lives of hundreds of African American citizens.

light. When Jesus used violence to cleanse the temple of the profiteers, He was in fact defending God's Holy Temple.

Love of freedom is a natural gift from God. This gift is embedded in the hearts of every living creature. You cage a bird and the bird ceases to be its God given self. You cage a human and he ceases being a human because a human must give free flight to the mind and body as a parallel to God's creation. After all, we are created in God's image.

Love of others will keep us concerned about the moral and physical well being of them. In our concern for them morally, we should do what we can to prevent them from committing sins against us. To allow them to treat us as anything less than children of God is to be a party to their sins. So you see if you love them you will do everything in your power to prevent them from convincing you to co-sin with them in your own oppression.

Love of self, means you can take inventory of self and still have high self-esteem in spite of what you uncover. It means you will glorify your God and life and defend your right to enjoy it. Let's get it together.

WHAT DO WE WANT?
We want land, power, and other resources.

Land and power equal freedom. One of the first things Yahweh did for the Israelites after they received reparations and departed Egypt was to provide land and power to them. He gave them the land of Canaan. In 1947 the converted European Jews acquired a homeland of their own. This has made a tangible difference in the lives of many Jews of the Diaspora. They feel more secure now that they have a homeland they can return to any time they desire. The host can make you feel at home or influence you to feel alienated to the point of consistently feeling like the "other," or Ralph Ellison's "invisible man." Having your own home to go to, gives you a different perspective and consequently a different reaction to a rude host.

When you are homeless, you are at the mercy of others and are usually treated accordingly.

There was an opportunity for the U.S government to do what was right for our landless and destitute ex-slave ancestors immediately following emancipation. Our ancestors desired land because they knew land, labor, and capital was the basis of freedom. Land was one of the main things the government and those who wanted to help should have provided if they were sincere in providing freedom for them. Dr Lerone Bennett provides the following insight on this tragedy.

> The Freedmen's Bureau and heroic New England school ma'am satisfied the hunger for letters. But no one-and this is the great tragedy of Reconstruct-ion - no one satisfied the hunger for land.[117]

Land is the basis of wealth. We can derive food, shelter, and resources, and a sense of security from our own creativity, and effort. Without it we are at the mercy of the white landowners and the white owners of capital. It is this understanding from experience gained since the beginning of time, that gave our captive ancestors the hunger for some land of their own.

This hunger for a land of our own has flowed continuously in our history.[118] It was the hunger of the individuals immediately following slavery on to Marcus Garvey, to the Republic of New Afrika, to the nation of Islam, various other groups, and millions of our Black people.

This hunger for land was consistently the focus of our ancestors who realized that the ownership of fertile land was their ticket out of poverty. They also believed the land they had worked and spilled their blood in for centuries without receiving

---

[117] Lerone Bennett. *Before the Mayflower* (New York: 1975) p. 188.
[118] See evidence of this in the testimony of Henry Adams, representative of African Americans in the next chapter.

the fruits of their labor was rightfully theirs. Dr. W.E.B. Dubois points out for our edification,

> Again and again, crudely but logically, the Negroes expressed their right to the land and the deep importance of this right. And as usual here the government played fast and loose because it had two irreconcilable ideas in mind. Thaddeus Stevens and Charles Sumner were perfectly clear; the Negroes must have land furnished them either for a nominal sum or as a gift, and this land should be furnished by the government and paid for either out of taxation, or as Stevens repeatedly insisted, as an indemnity placed on the South for Civil War. Moreover, for 250 years the Negroes had worked this land, and by every analogy in history, when they were emancipated the land ought to have belonged in large part to the workers.[119]

The "freed" slaves may have had the iron shackles that locked him in chattel slavery removed, but because they had no land or money, they ended up evolving into slaves of the new plantation owners. The old slave plantation syndrome has evolved into the new slave urban ghettoes. The only times we are peacefully allowed out is to leave for work at the new plantations and to spend what little money we have somehow come into possession of with the merchants.

We need land because land is the basis of wealth. It is from the land that we get food and mineral resources. When we have land we can use it for the common good of humanity.

We should have land because we worked the land for two and a half centuries and by right the land is ours. We should have land because we are unwelcome in the land (U.S.A) of our

---

[119] Dubois, W.E.B. *Black Reconstruction*. N.Y.:1935, p.368.

captivity. We are still oppressed and treated worse than many non-citizens and white folk's pet dogs. As recent as the year 2000, this point has been driven home for us. There was a big news media event in March of that year about an irate driver who threw someone's dog into oncoming traffic, which resulted in the dog's death. The emotional and moral outrage displayed by our white oppressors was understandable. Shortly thereafter, an Asian male tied his dog to the rear of his automobile and dragged him for many blocks. This also outraged our white oppressors. Now, I recall when the media displayed Rodney King being unmercifully beaten by several policemen, many white Americans cheered. When the African American male was tied to the back of a truck by several white racists and dragged to his death, there was no visible show of emotional and moral outrage by those same white folk. What's up with this attitude? What is it about the white oppressor and his love for his dog over and against their hatred of African Americans? If my reading and understanding of the Bible is correct, I believe Yahweh made man the steward of the earth and all else that occupy it, and commanded us (man) to love one another. Am I wrong? There is something ontologically wrong with the black / white relationship in this world.

Many times the courts of justice oppress and make unjust decisions against us. We are still the last hired and the first fired. We are still considered less than their pet dogs. Is this what you want? Does this situation induce joy or sadness in you? Wouldn't you rather have your own land somewhere?

Until the land issue is resolved, we will remain in the dependent and subjected economic situation that we are currently experiencing. However, if we could acquire enough land we could defend and call our own (politically), plus the capital to invest and enhance the economic production of that land, we could become independent and potentially as powerful and prosperous as any other nation. Without land, capital, and labor we will never become independent and self-sufficient.

Chapter 2

OUR HUNGER FOR LAND

The Testimony of Henry Adams
A Leader of "The Committee" Consisting of Representative African American Preachers and Laymen of The African Community in the U.S.A.

Before the U.S. Senate in 1880 Concerning
The Exodus of Blacks from the South.

Questions by Senator Winton
-Now tell us, Mr. Adams, what, if anything, you know about the exodus of the colored people from the Southern to the Northern and Western States...
-Well, in 1870, I believe it was, or about that year, after I had left the Army - I went into the Army in 1966 and came out the last of 1669 - and went right back home again where I went from, Shreveport; I enlisted there, and went back there. I enlisted in the Regular Army, and then I went back after I came out of the Army. After we had come out, a parcel of we men that was in the Army and other men thought that the way our people had been treated during the time we was in service - we heard so much talk of how they had been treated and opposed so much and there was no help for it - that caused me to go into the Army at first, the way our people was opposed. There was so much going on that I went off and left it; when I came back it was still going one, part of it, not quite so bad as at first. So a

parcel of us got together and said that we would organize ourselves into a committee and look into affairs and see the true condition of our race, whether it was possible we could stay under a people who had held us under bondage or not. Then we did so and organized a committee.

-What did you call your committee?

-We just called it a committee, that is all we called it, and it remained so; it increased to a large extent, and remained so. Some of the members of the committee was ordered by the committee to go into every state in the South where we had been slaves there, and post one another from time to time about the true condition of our race, and nothing but the truth.

-Was the object of that committee at that time to remove your people from the South, or what was it?

-O, no, sir; not then; we just wanted to see whether there was any State in the South where we could get a living and enjoy our rights.

-What was the character of the information that they gave you?

-Well, the character of the information they brought to us was very bad, sir.

-In what respect?

-They said that in other parts of the country where they traveled through, and whet they saw they was comparing with what we saw and whit we had seen in the part where we lived; we knowed what that was; and they cited several things that they saw in their travels; it was very bird.

-Do you remember any of these reports that you got from members of your committee?

-They said in several parts where they was that the land rent was still higher there in that part of the country than it was where we first organized it, and the people was still being whipped, some of them, by the old owners, the men that had owned them as slaves, and some of them was being cheated out of their crops just the same as they was there.

-Was anything said about their personal and political rights in these reports, as to how they were treated about these?

-Yes; some of them stated that in some parts of the country where they voted they would be shot. Some of them said that if they voted the Democratic ticket, they would not be injured.

-But that they would be shot, or might be shot, if they voted the Republican ticket?

-Yes, sir.

-I am speaking now of the period from 1870 to 1874, and you have given us the general character of the reports that you got from the South; what did you do in 1874?

-Well, along in August sometime in 1874, after the white league sprung up, they organized and said this is a white man's government, and the colored men should not hold any offices; they were no good but to work in the fields and take what they would give them and vote the Democratic ticket. That's what they would make public speeches and sly to us and we would hear them. We then organized an organization called the colonization council.

-In what way did you propose to better your condition?

-We first organized and adopted a plan to appeal to the president of the United States and to Congress to help us out of our distress, or protect us in our rights and privileges.

-Well, what other plan had you?

-And if that failed, our idea was then to ask them to set apart a territory in the United States for us, somewhere where we could go and live with our families.

-You preferred to go of somewhere by yourselves?

-Yes.

-Well, what then?

-If that failed, our other object was to ask for an appropriation of money to ship us all to Liberia, in Africa; somewhere where we could live in peace and quiet.

-Well, and what after that?

-When that failed then our idea was to appeal to other governments outside of the United States to help us to get away from the United States and go there and live under their flag.

-Now, let us understand more distinctly, before we go any further, the kind of people who composed the association. The committee, as I understand you, runs composed entirely of laboring people?

-Yes, sir.

-Did it include any politicians of either color, white or black?

-No politicians didn't belong to it, because we didn't allow them to know nothing about it, because we was afraid that if we allowed the colored politician to belong to it, he would tell it to the Republican politicians, and from that the men that was doing all this to us would get hold or it. too, and then get after us.

-So you did not trust any politicians, white or black?

-No, we didn't trust any of them.

-That was the condition of things during the time the committee was at work in 1870 to 1874?

-Yes, that was the condition.

-Did you appeal again?

-After the appeal in 1874, we appealed when the time got so hot down there they stopped our churches from having meetings after nine o'clock at night. They stopped them from sitting up and singing over the dead, and so forth, right in the little town where we lived, in Shreveport. I know that to be a fact; and after they did all this and we saw it was getting so warm-killing our people over the whole country-there was several of them killed right down in our parish-then we appealed. Well, in that petition we appealed there, if nothing could be done to stop the turmoil and strife, and give us our rights in the South, we appealed then, at that time, for 1 territory to be set apart for us to which we could go and take our families and live in peace and quiet.

-About what time did you lose all hope and confidence that your condition, could be tolerated in the Southern States?

-Well, we never lost all hopes in the world until 1877.
-Not until 1877?
-No, sir. In 1877 we lost all hopes.
-Why did you lose all hope in that year?
-Well, we found ourselves in such condition that we looked around and we seed that there was no way on earth, it seemed, that we could better our condition there, and we discussed that thoroughly in our organization along in May. We said that the whole South- every State in the South- had got into the hands of the very men that held us slaves -from one thing to another-and we thought that the men that held us slaves as holding the reins of government over our heads in every respect almost, even the constable up to the governor. We felt we had almost as well be slaves under these men. In regard to the whole matter that was discussed, it came up in every council. Then we said there was no hope for us and we had better go."[120]

The above document shows without equivocation, the desire of our ancestors to acquire some of this earth to call their own. We must however, admit that some of us (African Americans) didn't want to leave the paternalism of our white oppressors just as some don't today. This group is usually composed of the ignorant ones who do not know any better or those whose love of the master supercedes their love for themselves, and many of our so-called "middle class," miss-educated, intellectual people who love the master and are satisfied with being less than the master's pet.

SAMPLE OF PETITIONS FOR LAND IN LOUISIANA
List of Applications for Government Lands by Freedmen in accordance with Circular No. 10 - Headquarters Bureau Refugees, Freedmen, Abandoned Lands, State of Louisiana, with detailed statement.

---

[120] U.S. SENATE HEARINGS, Vol. 8, No. 693, 1880

2. Names of applicants: James Morgan, Freedman. Residence and Date: New Orleans, La., September 8, 1865. Number of men: 1. Number of women: 1. Number of children: 0. Means: 1 horse cart & c., small amt. of corn & forage, $50 in money. Remarks: This applicant is a discharged soldier and desires (10) ten acres of ground or less located if possible on Metarie Ridge, Parish Jefferson.

9. Names of applicants: Lewis Clark, a Freedman. Residence and Date: New Orleans, La., Sept. 8th, 1865. Number of men: 6. Number of women: 0. Number of children: 1. Means: $200 cash capital. Remarks: This applicant desires (40) forty acres of land in any place where it can be given.

10. Names of applicants: Grandison Hunt for Freedmen. Residence and Date: Ranche Plantation, Sept. 1st, 1865, Parish Terrebonne, La. Number of men: 22. Number of women: 20. Number of children: 40 (twenty-five families total). Means: $1,200 - $1,500 capital. Remarks: The applicant desires the whole of the Ranche Plantation (800 acres), Parish of Terrebonne.

11. Names of applicants: Grandison Hunt for Freedmen. Residence: Woodlawn Plantation, Parish Terrebonne, La., Sept. 1st, 1865. Number of men: 40. Number of women: 33. Number of children: 75 (36 families total). Means: $3 to 5,000, 30 mules and horses. Remarks: The applicant desires to have the whole of the Woodlawn Plantation (3,000 acres), Terrebonne, La.

12. Names of applicants: Grandison Hunt for Freedmen. Residence: Wm. Besland Plantation, Parish Terrebonne, La., and Sept. 1st, 1865. Number of men: 44. Number of women: 37. Number of children: 47 (44 families total). Means: $2,000 capital. Remarks: The applicant desires to lease the whole of the Wm. Besland Plantation (800 acres) Parish, Terrebonne, Louisiana

BLACK TOWNS AND SETTLEMENTS

The African American hunger for land motivated them to develop black townships in various localities in the United States and Canada. Morris Turner has written a well-documented book, *America's Black Towns and Settlements*, in which he has researched black towns and settlements. His research has uncovered over 200 such developments during the past century.

> The more than 200 black towns and settlements identified in this book represent only a fraction of the communities that once existed. Certainly further research is warranted, and it is the responsibility of African Americans, as well as others, to excavate and preserve the treasured legacy of these nearly forgotten pioneers.[121]

There were towns in Alaska, Alabama, Arkansas, California, Colorado, Connecticut, Florida, Georgia, Idaho, Illinois, Indiana, Kansas, Kentucky, Louisiana, Maine, Maryland, Massachusetts, Michigan, Minnesota, Mississippi, Missouri, Nebraska, Nevada, New Hampshire, New Jersey, New Mexico, New York, North Carolina, North Dakota, Ohio, Oklahoma, Pennsylvania, South Carolina, Tennessee, Texas, Utah, Virginia, Washington, West Virginia, Wisconsin and Canada.[122]

We have always wanted land as is evidenced by the above petitions by ex-slaves to acquire land in Louisiana, and the hundreds of towns and settlements created by African Americans. We needed land then and we need land now. We must realize we can't even feed ourselves; our oppressors furnish this basic necessity. We still stand in need of occupying

---

[121] Turner, Morris. *America's Black Towns and Settlements*. Rohnert Park, CA: 1998, p.9.
[122] See Turner's book.

some dirt we can call our own, and live our lives the way Yahweh desires us to.

> This land hunger – this absolutely fundamental and essential thing to any real emancipation of the slaves was continually pushed by all emancipated Negroes and their representatives in every Southern State. It was met by ridicule, by anger, and by dishonest and insincere efforts to satisfy it apparently.[123]

Ridicule was heaped on the idea because many high ranking power brokers had set the stage for the mass of white people to view Africans as less than human and inferior to white people. This propaganda was spread by the architect of the declaration of independence, the constitution of the USA and its President, Thomas Jefferson. John C. Calhoun and Samuel Cartwright also helped spread this satanic ideology to white racist population.

---

[123] W.E.B. DuBois. Black Reconstruction. Pg. 601.

Chapter 3

THE PROMISE

THE 40 ACRE DOCUMENTS
Special Field Orders. No.15 Hdqrs. Mil, Div. Of the Mississippi. In the Field, Savannah, Ga., January 16, 1865,

I. The islands from Charleston south, the abandoned ricefields along the rivers for thirty miles back from the sea, and the country bordering the Saint John's River, Fla., are reserved and set apart for the settlement of the negroes now made free by the acts of war and the proclamation of the President of the United States.

II. At Beaufort, Hilton Head, Savannah, Fernandina, Saint Augustine and Jacksonville the blacks may remain in their chosen or accustomed vocations; but on the islands, and in the settlements hereafter to be established, no white person whatever, unless military officers and soldiers detailed for duty, will be permitted to reside; and the sole and exclusive management of affairs will be left to the freed people themselves, subject only to the United States military authority and the acts of Congress. By the laws of war and orders of the President of the United States, the negro is free, and must be dealt with as such. He cannot be subjected to conscription or forced military service, save by the written orders of the highest military authority of this Department, under such regulations as the President or Congress may prescribe; domestic servants, blacksmiths, carpenters, and other mechanics will be free to

select their own work and residence, but the young and able-bodied negroes must be encouraged to enlist as soldiers in the service of the United States, to contribute their share toward maintaining their own freedom and securing their rights as citizens of the United States. Negroes so enlisted will be organized into companies, battalions, and regiments, under the orders of the United States military authorities, and will be paid, fed, and clothed according to law. The bounties paid on enlistment may, with the consent of the recruit, go to assist his family and settlement in procuring agricultural implements, seed, tools, boats,
clothing, and other articles necessary for their livelihood.

III. Whenever three respectable negroes, heads of families shall desire to settle on land, and shall have selected for that purpose an island or a locality clearly defined within the limits above designated, the inspector of settlements and plantations will himself, or by such subordinate officer as he may appoint, give them a license to settle such island or district, and afford them such assistance as he can to enable them to establish a peaceable agricultural settlement. The three parties named will subdivide the land, under the supervision of the inspector, among themselves and such others as may choose to settle near them, so that each family shall have a plot of not more than forty acres of tillable ground, and when it borders on some water channel with not more than 800 feet water front, in the possession of which land the military authorities will afford them protection until such time as they can protect themselves or until Congress shall regulate their title. The quartermaster may, on the requisition of the inspector of settlements and plantations, place at the disposal of the inspector one or more of the captured steamers to ply between the settlements and one or more of the commercial points, heretofore named in orders, to afford the settlers the opportunity to supply their necessary wants and to sell the products of their land and labor.

IV. Whenever a negro has enlisted in the military service of the United States he may locate his family in any one of the settlements at Pleasure and acquire a homestead and all other rights and privileges of a settler as though present in person. In like manner negroes may settle their families and engage on board the gun boats, or in fishing, or in the navigation of the inland waters, without losing any claim to land or other advantages derived from this system. But no one, unless an actual settler as above defined, or unless absent on Government service, will be entitled to claim any right to land or property in any settlement by virtue of these orders.

V. In order to carry out this system of settlement a general officer will be detailed as inspector of settlements and plantations, whose duty it shall be to visit the settlements, to regulate their police and general management, and who will furnish personally to each head of a family, subject to the approval of the President of the United States, a possessory title in writing, giving as near as possible the description of boundaries, and shall adjust all claims or conflicts that may arise under the same, subject to the like approval, treating such titles altogether as possessory. The same general officer will also be charged with the enlistment and organizaton of the negro recruits and protecting their interests while absent from their settlements, and will be governed by the rules and regulations prescribed by the War Department for such purpose.

VI. Brig. Gen. R. Saxton is hereby appointed inspector of settlements and plantations and will at once enter on the performance of his duties. No change is intended or desired in the settlement now on Beaufort Island, nor will any rights to Property heretofore acquired be affected thereby.

"By order of Maj. Gen. W.T. Sherman:
    L. M. DAYTON
    Assistant Adjutant-General

AN ACT TO ESTABLISH A BUREAU FOR THE RELIEF OF FREEMEN AND REFUGEES

Be it enacted by the Senate and House of Representatives of the United States of America in Congress assembled, That there is hereby established in the War Department, to continue during the present war of rebellion and for one year thereafter, a bureau of refugees, freedmen, and abandoned lands, to which shall be committed, as hereinafter provided, the supervision and management of all abandoned lands, and the control of all subjects relating to refugees and freedmen from rebel states, or from any district of country within the territory embraced in the operations of the army, under such rules and regulations as may be prescribed by the head of the bureau and approved by the President. The said bureau shall be under the management and control of a commissioner to be appointed by the President, by and with the advice and consent of the Senate, whose compensation shall be three thousand dollars per annum, and such number of clerks as may be assigned to him by the Secretary of War, not exceeding one chief clerk, two of the fourth class, two of the third class, and five of the first class. And the commissioner and all persons appointed under this act, shall, before entering upon their duties, take the oath of office prescribed in an act entitled "An ad to Prescribe an oath of office and for other purposes, "approved July second, eighteen hundred and sixty-two, and the commissioner and chief clerk shall, before entering upon their duties, give bonds to the treasurer of the United States, the former in the sum of fifty thousand dollars, and the latter in the sum of ten thousand dollars, conditioned for the faithful discharge of their duties respectively, with securities to be approved as sufficient by the the Attorney General, which bonds shall be filed in the office of the first comptroller of the treasury, to be by him put in suit for the benefit of any injured party upon any breach of the conditions thereof.

Sec. 2. And be it further enacted, That the Secretary of War may direct such issues of provisions, clothing, and fuel, as he may deem needful for the immediate and temporary shelter and supply of destitute and suffering refugees and freedmen and their wives and children, under such rules and regulations as he may direct.

Sec.3. And be it further enacted, That the resident may, by and with the advice and consent of the Senate, appoint an assistant commissioner for each of the states declared to be in insurrection, not exceeding ten in number, who shall, under the direction of the commissioner, aid in the execution of the provisions of this act; and he shall give a bond to the 'treasurer of the United States, in the sum of twenty thousand dollars, in the form and manner prescribed in the first section of this act. Each of said commissioners shall receive an annual salary of two thousand and five hundred dollars in full compensation for all his services. And any military officer may be detailed and assigned to duty under this act without increase of pay or allowances. The commissioner shall, before the commencement of each regular session of congress, make full report of his proceedings with exhibits of the state of his accounts to the President, who shall communicate the same to congress, and shall also make special reports whenever required to do so by the President or either house of congress; and the assistant commissioners shall make quarterly reports of their proceedings to the commissioner, and also such other special reports as from time to time may be required   Sec. 4. And be it further enacted, That the commissioner, under the direction of the President, shall have authority to set apart, for the use of loyal refugees and freedmen, such tracts of land within the insurrectionary states as shall have been abandoned, or to which the United States shall have acquired title by confiscation or sale, or otherwise, and to every male citizen, whether refugee or freedman, as aforesaid, there shall be assigned not more than forty acres of such land, and the person to whom it was so assigned shall be protected in the use and enjoyment of the land for the term of three years at an annual rent not exceeding six per cent upon the value of such land, as it was appraised by the state authorities in the year eighteen hundred and sixty, for the purpose of taxation, and in case no such appraisal can be found, then the rental shall be based upon the estimated value of the land in said year, to be ascertained in such manner as the commissioner may by regulation prescribe. At the end of said term, or at any time during said term, the occupants of any parcels so assigned may purchase the land and receive such title thereto as the United States can convey, upon paying therefor the value of the land, as ascertained and fixed for the purpose of determining the annual rent aforesaid.

Sec. 5. And be it further enacted, that all acts and parts of acts inconsistent with the provisions of this act, are hereby repealed.
Approved, March 3, 1865.
This act was passed by Congress and vetoed by President Andrew W. Johnson, on Feb 19, 1866.

Chapter 4

THE BETRAYAL

PRESIDENT JOHNSON'S VETO MESSAGE.

Washington, February 19, 1866.
To the Senate of the United States:

"I have examined with care the bill, which originated in the Senate and has been passed by the two Houses of congress, to amend an act entitled "An act to establish a bureau for the relief of freedmen and refugees," and for other purposes. Having with much regret come to the conclusion that it would not be consistent with the public welfare to give my approval to the measure, I return the bill to the Senate with my objections to its becoming a law..."

THE COMPROMISE OF 1877
The Straw That Broke the Camel's Back

Both of the presidential candidates, Hayes and Tilden (before the election), promised to restore "home rule" to the South. Both candidates also promised to withdraw federal support from the Reconstruction governments of Louisiana, South Carolina, and Florida.

Hayes won the presidency and the south became the beneficiary of a kept promise from him that all government troops would be removed from Florida, Louisiana and South Carolina, the federal government provided funds for a transcontinental railroad, and he appointed a southerner to his cabinet.

In the end, most of the land allocated to our freed ancestors was taken from them and given back to the slave landowners from whom they had initially confiscated the land. The initial struggle of our ancestors to receive justice and the promise of forty acres continues to be an inherent part of our continuing struggle today.

The following are a few of the larger organizations of African Americans that have committed themselves to the task of bringing the past due bill to the attention of many African Americans as, well as, white people and to acquiring a separate political homeland:

Chapter 5

GROUPS FOR REPARATIONS/LAND

INTERNATIONAL LEVEL

AFRICAN REPARATIONS MOVEMENT
ARM (UK) believes that people of African origin have an historic task to perform, that is to ensure that the truth of what happened to people of African origin is exposed and that reparations are made to African people. The achievement of African people has been truly remarkable, and just as we have emancipated ourselves from enslavement, de-colonized ourselves from the British Empire, destroyed apartheid in South Africa and continue to progress in the world despite racism - Victory is certain!!

NATIONAL LEVEL

N'COBRA
N'Cobra is the acronym for National Coalition of Blacks for Reparations in America. It is an umbrella organization of various groups and individuals. Their approach to reparations is to teach and inspire the grass roots African Americans and the utilization of a legal format and other methods to realize their goal.

REPUBLIC OF NEW AFRICA

The RNA is a provisional government of African Americans. Its headquarters are in Louisiana. The following is a capsule of its intent. This plan calls for:

> A HOLDING ACTION IN THE NORTH, with armed black communities and campaigns for black control of black schools and for responsive black men in political office;

> B. A MAJOR DRIVE TO WIN BLACK STATE POWER in Mississippi, where a near - majority of black people live, followed by similar drives for black control in Louisiana, Alabama, Georgia and South Carolina to create a five-state black union, a new nation, a NEW SOCIETY, free from racism, exploitation, and organized crime, based on brotherhood and justice and where everyone may attain his finest potentialities;

> C. A RIGOROUS MILITARY CAMPAIGN, run first by the black underground army and then by the county sheriff's machinery, as the counties come under black. Control, to destroy the white racist capacity for violence at its source.[124]

NATION OF ISLAM

This nation of black religious believers proclaimed the need for land under the leadership of its founder the Honorable Elijah Muhammad, and continues under the current leadership of Minister Louis Farrakhan.

---

[124] Brother Imari. *War in America: The Malcolm X Doctrine* (Detroit 1968) p.62, 63.

This is the question asked most frequently by both the whites and the Blacks. The answers to this question I shall state as simply as possible.
(1). We want freedom. We want a full and complete freedom.

(4). We want our people in America whose parents or grandparents were descendants from slaves, to be allowed to establish a separate state or territory of their own--either on this continent or elsewhere. We believe that our former slave masters are obligated to provide such land and that the area must be fertile and minerally rich. We believe that our former slave masters are obligated to maintain and supply our needs in this separate territory for the next 20 to 25 years--until we are able to produce and supply our own needs.

Since we cannot get along with them in peace and equality, after giving them 400 years of our sweat and blood and receiving in return some of the worst treatment human beings have ever experienced, we believe our contributions to this land and the suffering forced upon us by white America, justifies our demand for complete separation in a state or territory of our own.[125]

NEWARK BLACK POWER
CONFERENCE JULY 1967
The following is the position of the national umbrella organization that was formed in the wake of the struggles of the 60's:

---

[125] *The Final Call.* Vol. 15 Num. 9. March 1, 1995, p.39.

Whereas the black people in America have been Systematically oppressed by their white fellow-Country men;

Whereas there is little prospect that this oppression can be terminated, peace-fully or otherwise, within the fore-seeable future;

Whereas the black people do not wish to be absorbed into the larger white community;

Whereas the black people in America find that their interests are in contradiction with those of white America;

Whereas the black people in America are psychologically handicapped by virtue of their having no national homeland;

Whereas the physical, moral, ethical, and esthetic standards of white American society are not those of black society and indeed do violence to the self-image of the black man;

Whereas black people were among the earliest immigrants to America, having been ruthlessly separated from their fatherland, and have made a major contribution to America's development, most of this contribution having been uncompensated, and

Recognizing that efforts are already well advanced for the convening of a Constitutional Convention for the purpose of revising the Constitution of the United States for the first time since America's inception, then

Be it resolved that the Black Power Conference initiate a national dialogue on the desirability of partitioning the U.S. into two separate and independent nations, one to be a homeland for white and the other a homeland for black Americans.

The preceding records show that we have a deep inner need to own some of this dirt on this earth to call our own. Our people have always known that land is the basic ingredient in the arsenal of survival on planet earth. It is from the land that food derives. The earth produces everything we need. This planet has been referred to since very ancient times as "mother earth," because she births us, feeds us, and shelters us. The importance of being in control of some productive dirt on this earth that we can call our own has never been obfuscated. We Need Power: Political Economic and Military Power, and we need capital: Money, tools, machinery and other resources, and we need land.

SECTION V

Chapter 1

REPARATIONS AND JUDEO-CHRISTIAN CONTEXT

The main sin, which the United States is guilty of perpetrating, is the toleration of injustice. This society claims to be organized to protect the rights of the oppressed, but most often it functions as a bulwark of protection and perpetuation for the privileges of the white citizens. If this type situation exists, the biblical perspective insists that the perpetrator is immediately under God's judgment. If there is someone who disagrees with the charge that, the United States government and its citizenry are guilty of practicing injustice against the African people since the Atlantic slave trade, must be mentally wandering in an altered state of reality.

Evidence of the vastness of the devastation brought in the wake of the bloody, oppressive, injustices can be gathered from historical documents, and from studying the psychology of the descendants of the slaves. We now believe that most of the negative non productive personality traits many white sociologist claim are rampant in our peoples lives are really elements of the legacy of slavery and the injustices perpetrated by white citizens and sanctioned by the United States government.

The Bible constantly projects justice as a basic attribute of God. Justice is also projected as an essential component in the personality arsenal of the supposed godly person. The assertion that *nations* should be organized to promote justice is equally projected and is a fundamental element in biblical religion. This is the case in the writings and teachings of the Hebrew prophets. The opening chapter of Isaiah contains a good example (1:10-26). The prophet boldly calls Jerusalem Sodom and Gomorrah (v. 10) because its inhabitants think the smell of incense and sacrifice at their temple worship (11-15) to be acceptable by God as a substitute for justice to those whom they oppressed (17). Vv. 20-24 is a lament over the city, which, polluted by injustice, is now about to receive the punishment it deserves from its enemies.

We note that the mainline white American denominations; Catholic, Episcopalian, Lutheran, Presbyterian, and etc, conduct elaborate worship and celebratory services, yet most nevertheless did not readily protest the holding of slaves by its members. As a general rule, the Catholic Church was heavily involved in slave profiteering during the Atlantic slave trade. Others were also involved but most information on the profit ventures of them is either suppressed or, it may have been negligent. Furthermore many of these same churches are still the most segregated of places at 11 am every Sunday morning. We must also remember that it was the church that elaborated the theology that justified the enslavement of millions of Africans and paved the way for the loss of up to 100 million of our ancestor's lives. Now, when we observe the white church performing elaborate worship and sacrifice to God, we note the similarity to the Hebrews Isaiah was addressing in the passage above.

The correct thing for white citizens and the United States government to do if the hand of God's wrath is to be delayed is to try and make atonement. One road to that atonement is to come to a point of experiencing guilt, confessing the sin and trying with the best effort to right the wrong that was done. When nations attempt to right a wrong done to another nation or group of people, the effort is called reparations.

Reparation means retribution, restitution, and restoration. It is an attempt to do right for the wrong that has been done. It is recognition that the victim needs to be made whole again. In the Bible one of the criteria for a criminal's rehabilitation is paying restitution to the victim. Whatever the victim has been deprived of is replaced. If a person of today is deprived of his belongings, he or she has a right to seek restitution in the civil claims court. If someone causes another person psychological damage, bodily harm or death, restitution can be received through the court system. This criterion is especially useful involving the victim's loss of life, labor, and property because it is an attempt at righting a wrong that has been done. Restitutions could include land, money, technology, and etc.

I must however, admit that as early as 1867, Thaddeus Stevens, a son of slave masters, attempted with HR 29 Bill* to secure reparations for freed slaves in the form of 40 acre parcels of confiscated confederate land.

This Bill however, was defeated. The slave master and his descendants were adamant in their refusal to seriously take into consideration the payment of reparations to the children of the slaves

In Western culture one of the criteria for a guilty person's rehabilitation from crime is paying restitution to the victim. Throughout the Old Testament, restitution was the basic formula for punishing thieves and criminals. Ancient people were very clear and just in their radical concept and practice of restitution. Reparation, retribution, restitution, and restoration are synonymous and interconnected terms. At their origin is the sense of making something like it was before you messed it up.

---

* See, appendix

Retribution

Vestiges of this tradition in its' radicalism can be noted in the Old Testament saying, "eye for eye, tooth for tooth (retribution)."[126] The ancients were very clear in their understanding of justice. For every act of crime there must be an opposite and equal act of justice. You take a life; you give your life. The tradition is sweeping in its coverage of the damages done to the other. It appears to include all negative changes (physical and psychological) suffered by the victim to be repaid in kind on the person of the perpetrator. In this instance restitution is paid as retribution to society.

This radical theology of retribution is carried over into the New Testament notably in Paul's letter to the Church at Galatia.*

> Do not be deceived, God is not mocked; for whatever a man sows, this he shall reap[127]

There is an up side to the "eye for eye" theology, which is; it's being a just standard for all people. Even if a rich man takes a life, he forfeits his own life. This is pure justice. It may have been primitive in its approach to justice, but we must admit the intent was pure justice in its implementation.

> Judges must always be just in their sentences, not noticing whether a person is poor or rich; they must always be perfectly fair.[128]

We are then assured, "There shall be one standard for all,"[129] this tradition underscores this claim and widen its coverage to

---

[126] *Leviticus* 24:20
* Galatia was a province in what is currently called Turkey.
[127] *Galatians* 6:7
[128] *Leviticus* 19:15. The Living Bible. Paraphrased. Holman Illus. Edit. New York: 1973.
[129] ibid. 24:22a

include everyone in the world with, "for the stranger as well as the native."[130] This is authoritative because the one who commands, tells us, "for I am the Lord your God."[131]

Though it is difficult for us to accept restitution in its Old Testament radical form, we must nevertheless admit it is just restitution for the victim, "Eye for eye, tooth for tooth, life for life". Jesus Christ came not to destroy the Law but to fulfill it. When we accept Him we are in Grace and not subject to the Law, but to be under this Grace we should have confessed Christ, which presupposes our repentance. Repentance involves forgiveness, which involves doing what is right, and returning stolen properties if we are guilty of thievery. In other words make a wholehearted effort to repair the damages we caused to our brother. Repentance is a prerequisite to forgiveness. For if there is no remorse (repentance), there is nothing to forgive. Forgiveness is received only by remorsefulness. Remorse should always include restitution. If a criminal is really sorry for his actions and its consequence, his remorse must be inextricably connected with correcting the wrong. If he broke it, he must take responsibility and fix it. Jesus commanded the 12 and 70 messengers to preach repentance.[132] John, who baptized Jesus, began his ministry preaching repentance.[133] Paul and Peter, early church fathers, also preached repentance.[134] It is impossible to be a Christian and fellowship with Yahweh and not repent of murder, torture, and exploitation.

Admission of guilt is denied by our government as well as many white citizens who are born with privileges derived from this system which was built on the initial profits derived from the blood, sweat, suffering, death and free labor of our ancestors. Whites and others derive wealth and privileges from

---

[130] ibid. 24:22b
[131] ibid. 24:22c
[132] *Luke* 24:47, Mark 6:12
[133] *Matthew* 3:1-2, 4:17.
[134] *Acts* 2:38, 20:21.

a system built on what was stolen from us. They all benefit from the economic fruits of our ancestor's stolen labor today and should be held partially responsible for the stolen labor bill.

Our white oppressors have taken the lives, damaged the minds and characters of millions of our people during the past approximately 400 years. Will Yahweh's word be implemented on them? Is Yahweh really immutable? Does His word change? Can we trust in His justice? As I stated earlier, I shudder for the future prospects of our white oppressors in the context of our justice providing God.

Restitution

The basic definition is to give back what was taken. Let us observe this tradition in one of its Old Testament forms. The following is a tradition in which God speaks to Moses about restitution

> THEN the Lord spoke to Moses, saying
> 2 "When a person sins and acts unfaithfully against the LORD, and deceives his companion in regard to a deposit or a security entrusted to *him*, or through robbery, or *if* he has extorted from his companion,
> 3 or has found what was lost and lied about it and sworn falsely, so that he sins in regard to anyone of the things a man may do;
> 4 then it shall be, when he sins and becomes guilty, that he shall restore what he took by robbery, *or* what he got by extortion, or the deposit which was entrusted to him, or the lost thing which he found,
> 5 or anything about which he swore falsely; he shall make restitution for it in full, and add to it one-fifth more. He shall give it to the one to whom

it belongs on the day he *presents* his guilt offering.[135]

This text informs us that the same reparation due for damage to God's property is demanded for one's neighbor-with the prerequisite of rectification with man can it be sought from God.

Restitution restoration, and reparation are synonymous terms. Restitution is the preferred religious term and reparation is civil.

Restoration
Jacob the Thief of Esau's Birthright, Meets Esau

In the morning Jacob saw Esau approaching with his band of four hundred men. Jacob separated the children of Leah and Rachel and the two handmaids, putting the handmaids and their children in front, then Leah and her children, and Rachel and Joseph last. Then he went on ahead and bowed to the ground seven times as he neared Esau. He did everything, humanly speaking, that he could do to appease his brother. However, nothing that he could have done would have saved him at this time if the Lord had not been with him and blessed him. But the Lord did intervene for him because of Jacob's willingness to make *restoration* to his brother when the Angel blessed him early that morning.

Esau had had a change of heart and ran to meet Jacob and embraced him. He wanted to know to whom all the women and children belonged, and Jacob told him that they were the children God had given to him. Then Esau asked about the droves, which he had met, Jacob replied, "These are to find grace in the sight of my lord."[136] In this statement, and by his act of bowing to Esau, Jacob returned the lordship (birthright)

---
[135] *Lev.* 6:1-5. New American Standard Bible. Thomas Nelson, N.Y: 1977.
[136] *Genesis* 33:8

that he had taken from his brother. He had received the lordship when he had deceived his father Isaac and stolen Esau's blessing. Jacob fulfilled the demand of the Lord when he was wrestling with the Angel. The Lord had brought him into favor with Esau because he had become willing to make that *restoration*.

Jesus implied in his response to Zaccheus' admission of restoring what he has gained through oppressing and exploiting others, that his act of restoration was an important factor in his experiencing salvation.

> And Zaccheus stood, and said unto the Lord; Behold, Lord, the half of my goods I give to the poor; and if I have taken any thing from any man by false accusation, I restore him fourfold.
> And Jesus said unto him, "This day is salvation come to this house, forasmuch as he also is a son of Abraham."[137]

In the tradition of the Old, as well as the New Testament, restoration was an important factor in the basic laws for correcting the wrongs done to others.

---

[137] *Luke* 19:8,9. Reference Passage Bible. Alpha Publishing Co. Lincoln, Nebraska: 1912.

Chapte2

EXODUS
REPARATIONS PARADIGM

The following text is taken from the story of God's deliverance of His people from Egypt. This story has served as a paradigm of what God (Yahweh) is doing in our oppressed lives. I can remember when I was just six years old hearing my father claim, "Just as God delivered His people from Pharaoh's hand, He is working our freedom out right now." We identified with Yahweh's people "Down in Egypt Land". That story is our story. As Yahweh works out our freedom, I also hope we learn from this paradigm that our freedom is tied to the reparations due us.
Let's take a look (Exod.11-12, 36).
It was to complete the Divine judgment upon Egypt (Exodus 13:12), and also finally to compel Pharaoh and his people to "Let My people Go." Yahweh declared that He would Himself destroy "every first-born in the land of Egypt, from the first-born of man to the first-born of beasts." The time fixed for the last plague was midnight on the fourteenth of the month which had already started, and which was to be observed by the Israelites as the first month of their sacred year. Each Israelite household was (I) to select, a lamb or goat, one year old and without blemish, on the tenth of the month; (2) to slay it on the fourteenth, just before twilight, and to sprinkle some of its blood on the door posts of each house, and (3) on the same evening, before midnight, to eat it quickly with unleavened

bread and bitter herbs, with their clothes on, their shoes on their feet, and their stakes to secure the tents in hand, like people in a hurry to depart. The children of Israel obeyed these Divine orders, and at midnight on the fourteenth of the month of Abib, Yaweh *passed over* the houses, which He saw marked with blood, and destroyed all the first-born in the land of Egypt.

The tenth plague was 1, an implementation of divine power on behalf of Israel, and 2; it also displayed Divine judgment upon Pharaoh and his people. God allowed no one to escape his judgment because of the defense statements "I never owned any slaves," or, "That was a long time ago" or, "You Israelites need to get over it, and get on with your lives." No, God didn't listen to any of it. He sent death to the first born of everyone who was not covered by the blood of the sacrifice.

Pharaoh was filled with fear and terror by the awful blow Yahweh had dealt to every Egyptian family. Pharaoh and the Egyptians tried to persuade the Israelites to depart at once. The Bible informs us that when they left Egypt, the Israelites were "about 600,000 men besides children," which makes it probable that they formed a body of emigrants which approximated a couple millions people. This large number makes it difficult to imagine how the entire Hebrew nation could leave under the conditions as set forth in the narration in the Bible. Together with their *national freedom*, the Israelites received many valuable gifts as *reparations* from the Egyptians. Moses had instructed them that on the night of the exodus, they should ask for *silver* and *gold jewels*, and *clothing* from their oppressors, and amidst the excitement, produced by the tenth plague, each Egyptian household gave the Israelites everything they asked for. They provided very valuable things, but regardless of how precious, they were merely a small *compensation* secured by God to His people for the four centuries of their stolen and *unpaid labor*.

We can easily discern that it was *reparations* the Egyptians gave to the departing Children of Israel and not a deceptive *borrowing* without the intent of paying the loan back as some interpreters would have it. Because the King James Version uses the word "borrow" in connection with the instructions to obtain jewels and other gifts from the Egyptians, many have questioned the honesty of God's people in this instance. This interpretation is not likely because this would also implicate God as participating in the dishonesty. This calls for an interpretation and depiction of God deceiving, lying, stealing, and appearing hypocritical especially, since in Exodus 20:15, He explicitly commands them, "Thou shalt not steal." In Leviticus 19:13, the command is, "Thou shalt not defraud thy neighbor, neither rob him." However, the Hebrew word translated as borrow (*shaal*) literally means "to ask for," so Israel was not instructed to borrow in the meaning of the word today. It was rather, an asking for what was naturally theirs; the fruits of their labors.

God made the promise of *reparations* for his people to Moses in Exodus 3:21,22, and His promise for *reparations* was fulfilled in Exodus 12:35,36.

When God allowed the Hebrews to obtain *reparations* from their oppressors of 400 years, He was merely fulfilling a promise He made to Moses as he directed him to go down in Egypt land and tell Pharaoh to let His people go. Read what God promised to do for the Hebrews.

> And I will give this people favor in the sight of the Egyptians; and it shall come to pass, that, when you go, ye shall not go empty
>
> But every woman shall borrow of her neighbour, and of her that sojourn in her house, jewels of silver, and jewels of gold, and raiment: and ye shall put them upon your sons, and upon

your daughters; and ye shall spoil the Egyptians.[138]

In the first verse, God promises Moses that the oppressors would view the oppressed with favor. In other words these formerly despised slaves were going to be viewed differently then, by the Egyptians. They were to be "looked upon with favor." This would be similar to our current oppressors, who view us as "heathens" "monkeys," "niggers", negroes, or "coloreds" to suddenly view us as blessed by God and protected by His Almighty Righteousness. The Egyptians would surely have experienced a change of heart to change their opinion of their "niggers" to that of being "Blessed of God." They would have come to a place in their relationship with the Hebrews where their view of them as slaves would change to understanding them as their brothers and consequently experience guilt for what they had done to them. The whole master/slave relationship dynamics would change because they would have come to realize what they had done all those years to the Hebrews was wrong. God through his judgment on them would bring them to a state of remorse. In their search for remorsefulness they would come to realize that one of its conditions was the freedom of the Hebrews.

In that same verse God promised, "when ye go, ye shall not go empty." God promised not only to cause the oppressors to view them with favor, but He also promised in the same breath that when they received their liberation and leave the oppressor's land they would not leave empty handed but with some sort of compensation for their stolen labor during enslavement.

God proceeded to tell Moses the method they were to utilize in acquiring some degree of compensation for their stolen labor of approximately 400 years. "Every woman shall borrow

---

[138] *Exodus* 3:21,22.

(demand, or ask for, according to the Hebrew word) from the Egyptian women, all her friends and visitors gold, silver and clothing".

They were not to use this compensation for themselves but were to give it as an *inheritance* to their sons and daughters. God knew that freedom with empty hands meant continued slavery and degradation for the descendants of the Hebrews, so He promised the enslaved Hebrews *reparations* with their freedom as an inheritance for their children. On our ancestors supposed day of freedom they were as empty handed as the day before. No *reparations* were forth coming and they had to enter a supposed freedom, begging or stealing food to eat and with no payment for their stolen labor to pass down to their children. We are still waiting on our reparations and the inheritance for our children

Our ancestors identified with the exodus story, it became their paradigm for freedom. They were aware that the Hebrews, who left Egypt, departed towards freedom with reparations. This is betrayed in that old African American Spiritual, "Go Down Moses". Verse three of this once popular song is as follows.

> No more shall they in bondage toil, Let my people go
> Let them come out with Egypt's spoil, Let my people go.[139]

There is no doubt that our ancestors meant reparations in using the Biblical term "spoil." The use of the word "spoil' is dependant on the word toil with which it rhymes, and corresponds. Black people were really singing about their own predicament and this third line reflects their expectation of receiving reparations for their toil in bondage.

---

[139] *Songs of Zion*. Nashville:1981.p.112

Now, because God is immutable (unchanging) and just and intended the oppressed Hebrews to receive back pay for their stolen labor surely, He wants Africans to receive what is due them. God cannot be a respecter of persons or nations. He can't want justice for the Hebrews and not for us. We believe in a God who provides, protects, and is just, to all people.

When the Hebrews presented the Egyptians with a bill for their stolen labor, everybody paid because Egypt was in fear and stood in disarray from the last plague. God had commanded His people through Moses, to demand the *gold*, *silver* and *cloths* from every Egyptian home. According to His promise they were to receive so much *reparations* it would spoil (damage) the Egyptian economy.

If this story of God working in the Hebrews liberation is to continue being the paradigm we model our struggle after, then of necessity we must be willing to demand and expect *reparations* from the oppressors up to the place where it *spoils* their economy. We too, have been enslaved, robbed of our labor, and we likewise need compensation to pass on to our children.

Chapter 3

REDRESS FOR STOLEN LABOR

James, the brother of Jesus Christ, wrote the epistle of James. Various scholars have defined this epistle as a revolutionary tract. As is easily noted, James, like his brother Jesus was definitely a champion of the oppressed.

> COME now, you rich, weep and howl for your miseries which are coming upon you.
> 2 Your riches have rotted and your garments have become moth-eaten.
> 3 Your gold and your silver have rusted; and their rust will be a witness against you and will consume your flesh like fire. It is in the last days that you have stored up your treasure!
> 4 Behold, the pay of the laborers who mowed your fields, *and* which has been withheld by you, cries out *against you;* and the outcry of those who did the harvesting has reached the ears of the Lord of Sabbath.
> 5 You have lived luxuriously on the earth and led a life of wanton pleasure; you have fattened your hearts in a day of slaughter.
> 6 You have condemned and put to death the righteous *man;* he does not resist you.[140]

---

[140] *James* 5:1-6

James simply says to the economic oppressor, those from whom you stole labor have cried to the Lord and He hears them. Don't you know that God will hear us if we cry out to Him? We cry out to God as we engage in struggle for him to guide, protect and provide us with justice. James is reiterating what the writer of Leviticus proclaims.

> You shall not rob or oppress anyone, and you shall pay your hired workers promptly. If something is due them, don't keep it overnight.[141]

When I consider Yahweh is a just God and His word claim, "You shall reap, what you sow," I know that the judgment is that we receive in direct proportion to what we have done. The future of our white oppressors is bleak indeed if they are to receive in direct proportion to what they have sown on our ancestors during chattel slavery and on us today.

Reconciliation makes things the way they were, it recreates wholeness with the other by making your relationship right with them. Jesus Christ tells us God will not accept man's offerings if he has caused a breach between another person and himself. It logically follows that if our oppressors want to be reconciled to God they must first become reconciled with us. The white nation cannot be reconciled to us until we forgive them for their evil transgressions against us. We, on the other hand, cannot forgive them until they first admit their transgressions and ask for our forgiveness. How can we forgive the robber unless he admits his guilt and gives us back what he has stolen from us? As a matter of fact when we confront them about their historically, oppressive actions against us and the pain we still suffer as a result, they begin that popular refrain, "I never

---

[141] *Leviticus* 19:13

owned any slaves, you people need to get over something that happened so long ago and get own with your lives."

No individual citizen can completely escape responsibility for the actions or inactions of the nation or race to which he or she belongs. This is thoroughly grounded in the Christian faith. The major premise of the Christian faith is the concept of our need for salvation from something God placed on us because of the actions of our first parents in the Garden of Eden.

Some biblical writers condemned whole nations without differentiating between the guilty and the supposed innocent citizen.*

Many white citizens are too blind to realize that their special privileges today derive from our historical suffering and our ancestors stolen labor. Maybe they don't want to face the awful sins their ancestors, government and many of them commit against us even today. But, how can they ever reconcile themselves to God and us until they repent of their horrible sins?

Our moral and human sense cries out for God to intervene for the horrific crimes committed against our ancestors. However, many of us for whatever reason don't believe the United States will ever repay us for our stolen inheritance or for the pain and suffering we still experience as a legacy of slavery. We must demand for the sake of our dignity and our future well being that what was stolen must be returned us. Besides, we owe it to our white American brothers and sisters to try and provide a platform on which we can facilitate reconciliation with them.

We must learn to look to our God and emulate his behavior. Aren't we supposed to reflect God in our lives? Doesn't God require repentance as a prerequisite for forgiveness? We should too. Reconciliation involves forgiveness. How can we forgive them if they don't repent? How can they expect it while they are

---

* *Nahum* 3:1-7; *Obadiah* 1:8-14,21; *Lamentations* 1:1-9.

in denial of needing it? Can we forgive, I mean truly forgive and help bring about the necessary healing that is needed, without their repentance? Can they experience repentance without fixing the damage they have caused, or at least received privileges derived from our pain and brokenness?

We are struggling for justice while the oppressor pretends he doesn't understand why we can't forget about our holocaust and get on with our lives. He acts as though he has no understanding of the primary role his acknowledgment of our pain and suffering has in our becoming well again. He pretends not to understand that most of our current problems result as direct consequences of his evilness. His show of remorsefulness would contribute greatly to our transcending the dynamics of slavery and getting on with the healing process.

We are due an apology from the highest U.S. governmental level and a sincere attempt by those who are guilty (U.S. Government, American Indians, Jews, Arabs, some European Governments, Churches and Synagogues) to pay us back for stealing the rightful inheritance we should have received from our ancestors, and repair the damages they are responsible for, so we can have peace and true fellowship.

We qualify for reparations (repairs) based on three facts:

One, an unjust war has been perpetrated against us by agents such as hate mobs, small terrorist groups sanctioned by the United States government, National Guard, and the Armed Forces. The history of the many attacks on us by the preceding groups can easily be documented in current history books.

Second, we are due punitive damages for the torture and suffering our ancestors endured, and the mental and physical suffering we still experience as a result of the continuing legacy of slavery.

Third, we are due the inheritance of the labor of our ancestors. Their labor was stolen and the fruits of it were used for the benefit of capitalism and other people. All resources that resulted from their labor should have been theirs to use to improve their lives spiritually and physically. Those improvements should have passed on down to us. The children of the masters are privileged and benefit most from the results of our ancestors' labor, while we the children of the slaves receive the leftovers. We must exercise some dignity and seek an apology from those who assaulted us and demand reparations. Otherwise, we will never have any respect for ourselves, and consequently other peoples will continue to disrespect us.

GOD'S JUDGMENT ON AMERICA

Ancient Israel[*] emphasized righteousness as the basic moral attribute of God. God, as revealed in the Christian Bible, can always be depended on to do what is right. He is not capricious, doing one thing today and another tomorrow. He also, always applies the same standards all people. He is defined as the perfect judge. His judgment is the inevitable place we all must stand in, and receive our just dues in direct proportion to the quality of the impact of our actions on other people's lives. The theme of His righteous judgment races relentlessly throughout the bible.

The entire moral life of the United States is deeply infected with the sins associated with injustices towards other humans (black race in particular), which depicts their personal disloyalty towards God. This is why God's judgment, of necessity must be on America if its government and people do not repent from their evil works. There are many passages of scripture that illustrate God's displeasure with injustice; we shall consider the prophecy of Amos regarding God's judgment on nations with similar practices of injustice as the United States does today.

There appears to be several categories of crimes noted by Amos against the nations. His fellow citizens agreed with his scathing pronouncements about God's judgment on their enemies. That's the way of humans. We can easily note the

---

[*] The use of the term ancient is meant to point to those persons who departed from and have their origin in Egypt and conquered Caanan, as opposed to the people who now occupy the land. These modern Jewish occupiers are from Europe and are descendants of the Khazars who converted to Judaism in the seventh century.

speck in someone else's eye, especially when we are focused on their shortcomings and not ours. White Americans can readily point to the evils of others. Note President Bush's recent "axis of evil," comments on some Islamic societies. Note his failure to look at and acknowledge the personal and corporate evils Americans are guilty of committing against Africans. Let us observe the charges against the "others," by Amos.

1. Cruelty: (Damascus, 1:3-5). Damascus was the capital of the Syrian empire, and had become weak during the time Amos spoke. However, her past crimes of atrocity are still remembered. This seems like a replica of the African American's remembrance of the past atrocities against them by the government and citizenry of the United States. In light of Amos' proclamation of God's judgment against Syrians for their past atrocities, white Americans and others should understand that their pretending that the Atlantic slave trade wasn't that bad or, "that was a long time ago," or " you people need to get over it, and get on with your lives," does not exempt them from the judgment of God. The Syrians have not had a monopoly on cruelty. The following news account of cruelty by white Americans to Africans exposes them as unequaled in their barbarous acts of cruelty. Even the ones their anthropologists and other scientists have defined as savages fail to measure up to the quality of cruelty that has been displayed by America on Africans for the entire world to witness.

> The annals of the savage will be searched in vain for anything worse than the exhibition given to the world by the white civilization of the state of Georgia. The best that the devilish ingenuity of man has ever been able to do, in any age or among any people, to make the ordeal of death as excruciating and awful as it could possibly be made, was equaled in the torture and mutilation

and burning of the negro Holt; and if any large company of human beings at any stage in the development of the race ever gave greater evidences of joy, in such a spectacle or rushed with greater eagerness to secure mementoes of the fearful tragedy in the form of pieces of the burned flesh and bits of the charred bones, history makes no record of the fact.[142]

If evilness can be defined as intentional pain inflicted on another human being, then we can confidently say without any serious opposition, that for an executioner to delay the victim's death, so that the optimum amount of pain will be experienced is a perpetration by Satan himself.

The nation and the whole civilized world must stand aghast at the revelation. A civilized community numbering thousands, at the drop of a hat, throws off the restraints and effects of many centuries of progress and stands forth in the naked savagery of the primitive man. Men and women cheer and express feelings of triumph and joy as the victim is hurried on to the stake to make a Sunday holiday in one of the most orthodox religious communities in the United States. They cut off his ears, his fingers and other members of the body, and strip him and pour oil upon him while the spectators crowd desperately for positions of advantage in the great work of torture and death. As the flames rise about the victim the people watch the quiverings of the flesh and the

---

[142] Editorial from; *The Springfield* (Massachusetts) *Weekly Republican*. April 28, 1899

> writhings of the fragile, and shout back descriptions to the jostling, cheering hundreds on the outskirts of the ring. The negro raises a cry of agony that can be heard far away, and in a supreme effort loosens the upper part of his body from the chain which binds it to the tree. The fire is deadened while he is being chained back, and the awful agony prolonged to the evident relish of the spectators. Then more oil and fire, and death at last comes to the man's release.[143]

Can God be for such behavior? If He is not for it then, He must be against it. Since God is the same yesterday, today and tomorrow. He is unchanging, in that He has never been, nor is He now, a respecter of persons. In Him there is no male-female, Jew-Gentile, rich-poor or black-white. The judgment He placed on Syria, Ammon, Babylon, Israel, Judah and others for their wickedness is the same judgment He places on modern nations that are guilty of the same kinds of evilness. He has to, or He stands exposed as a hypocrite and guilty of favoritism. However, God is just and to be just is in contradistinction to being partial.

Ammon, 1:13-15, is charged with viciously ripping open the abdomen of pregnant women and destroying the unborn children. In a sense you could say America is guilty of killing unborn children of African women. C.L.R. James provides the following claim about this beastly practice.

> The pregnant woman was not spared her "four posts. A hole was dug in the earth to accommodate the unborn child.[144]

---

[143] Ibid.
[144] CLR James. *The Black Jacobins*. N.Y.:1938. P.13.

The preceding example is one concerning pregnant African women during the horrible slave period being flogged while tied down and secured to four posts, one at each wrist and ankle. The unborn black child was aborted into a hole in mother earth.

2. Enslavement (Philistia 1:6-8), modern day Palestine was anciently charged with selling whole towns into slavery, and the Edomites acted as middlemen in this trade by transporting the slaves to the market places and reselling them. The similarity to the historical evidence that shows, various African kingdoms are guilty of capturing and selling entire villages into slavery is uncanny. And when we note that the Arabs and Europeans transported those African captives throughout the world and its various markets for resale, we began to believe the prophecy points to the judgment of modern day Africa, Europe and all others involved in the sale of those humans. They must all face the judgment of God. Perhaps that is one significant reason our beloved mother Africa is in the plight she's in. Judgment must come as sure as night follows day.

> --- 16 Therefore the Lord God of Hosts says this: "There will be crying in all the streets and every road. Call for the farmers to weep with you, too; call for professional mourners to wail and lament. 17 There will be sorrow and crying in every vineyard, for I will pass through and destroy. 18 You say, 'If only the Day of the Lord were here, for then God would deliver us from all our foes.' But you have no idea what you ask. For that day will *not* be light and prosperity, but darkness and doom! How terrible the darkness will be for you; not a ray of joy or hope will shine. 19 In that day you will be as a man who is chased by a lion-and met by a bear, or a man in a dark room who leans

> against a wall-and puts his hand on a snake. 20 Yes that will be a dark and hopeless day for you.
> 21 I hate your show and pretence-your hypocrisy of honoring' me with your religious feasts and solemn assemblies. 22 I will not accept your burnt offerings and thank offerings. I will not look at your offerings of peace. 23 Away with your hymns of praise- they are mere noise to my ears. I will not listen to your music, no matter how lovely it is."

The sins of the white man in racial matters have created a dilemma that threatens to shake this nation to its foundation and usher in its civilizational demise. This dilemma is birthed in the hope and aspirations of Africans to become all God created them to be, and the reality of white citizens and their government being bulwarks of resistance and oppression to those aspirations. American scholar, Andrew Hacker makes the following observation on the situation.

> The dilemma is quite obvious; Africans in the USA want the opportunity to manifest their total self-actualization. Whites in the USA have built their self-esteem on oppressing the black self.[145]

Because of the inevitable continuous evolving mental empowerment of the black race, their total thrust for spiritual and physical liberation will accelerate in the near future as white terror increases, and the elements for a most devastating conflagration can possibly be the key that opens the door to the destruction of America. That America will be judged in a devastating war is a fact that is established in the prophecies of God's ancient prophets.

---

[145] Andrew Hacker. *Two Nations. Black and White, Separate, Hostile, Unequal.* N.Y: 1992 P.229

3. Corporate Responsibility: No white person can completely escape responsibility for the actions of their government and nation. As much as some of us would like for it to be another way, children nevertheless do inherit the sins of the fathers. If this is not the case, then the biblical position of the original sin of Adam and Eve making us all guilty and standing in the need of redemption falls flat on its face. If we accept the fall of humans as resulting from the sins of the first parents, then of necessity we must accept the position of corporate guilt in white America for the past and present personal and national evils committed against our people.

In the book of Lamentations, we note that Zion, as a whole was counted as guilty and corrupt, not just it's guilty leaders and those whose actions made their guilt obvious. Everybody went down because the entire nation was judged guilty. The people suffered corporately for the sins of the fathers. Her "priests are groaning,"[146] her "virgins are afflicted,"[147] her "adversaries have become her masters,"[148] and her children "have gone away as captives before the adversary."[149]

So, you see corporate judgment was utilized when the nation as a whole was found guilty of the transgressions. That old routine quote, "I never owned any slaves, nor have I ever oppressed any black folk" will not help individual whites one iota. For the truth is, whatever the white slavers derived from the enslavement and torture of our people, was inherited by their children and their children, and whatever resulted from the slave system and inherited by the slaves, was inherited by their children and their children. We Africans today, carry the heavy baggage of inferiority, fear, anger, dependency, low self-esteem and other negative traits developed in and inherited as a legacy

---

[146] *Lamentations.* 1:4,5.
[147] Ibid.
[148] Ibid.
[149] Ibid. v.5

of slavery. Now, the white citizenry has inherited a highly developed economic system, and a legacy of guilt that has its ground of being in the institution of slavery. Individual whites may claim they feel no guilt, but God has judged America and found her guilty of committing horrific sins against African people.

Though, vengeance is the Lord's, and the judgment is the Lord's, when the final battle comes it will come partly out of our (black people) need for a mind cleansing retribution. The government and its scholars know it is almost impossible to do what has been done to us and not expect retribution. Many scholars make mention of racial memory. It is the eternal memory of the race's experiences throughout its past existence. It is this memory that pushes and pulls us towards making certain choices now. It has prompted us to laugh when there was nothing funny being said. It has invited many of us to a life of "Tomism." It has caused many thousands to choose flight over fight at the moment of decision. It has caused many others to remember their pain and turn that pain back to its place of origin. One glaring example of this is the example within the context of the Haitian slave revolution, led by the African priest, Boukman, against the white slave masters.

> From their masters they had known rape, torture, degradation, and, at the slightest provocation, death. They returned in kind. For two centuries the higher civilization had shown them that power was used for wreaking your will on those whom you controlled. Now that they held power they did as they had been taught. In the frenzy of the first encounters they killed all, yet they spared the priests whom they feared and the surgeons who had been kind to them. They, whose women had undergone countless violations, violated all the women who fell into their hands, often on the

> bodies of their still bleeding husbands, fathers and brothers. "Vengeance! Vengeance!" was their war-cry, and one of them carried a white child on a pike as a standard.[150]

The act of retribution is a liberating factor, and it is no accident that Christianity speaks of being washed in the blood as an act of liberation. Whites must become witnesses of the cross; they must suffer the death of the cross and become washed in its blood. Blacks on the other hand will become free of all white domination when whites bear the witness of the cross just as we have done in slavery, and today, with its many tortures and pains. The cross of Calvary is where voluntary suffering took place so that the world might be saved. The white man must go to the cross willingly, without uttering a murmuring word because this is the route to reconciliation between the black victim and the white oppressor. This is the road to absolve the vast accumulation of estrangement, guilt, shame and terror that so overwhelms the black/white relationship.

Destruction of America

The final war is already upon us claims some voices. It is however, viewed by one notable leader within the African community as a cosmic struggle.

> The final war between Allah (God) and the devils is dangerously close. The very least amount of friction can bring it into action within minutes. There is no such thing as getting ready for this most terrible and dreadful war; they are ready. Preparation for the battle between man and man or nations has been made and carried out on land and water for the past 6,000 years. Man has now

---

[150] C.L.R. James. *The Black Jacobians*. N.Y: 1962. P.88

> become very wise and has learned many of the secrets of nature which make the old battles with swords and bows and arrows look like child's play.[151]

It is essential that the white oppressor nation confront the evils committed by their ancestors and government against our ancestors and to us today. They must stop using the excuse "we didn't do it, it happened a long time ago. You people need to get over it." They must admit this evilness so the long deserved healing process can begin. If we are to be healed it is important that our historical oppressor be a part of the process. How can there be peace as long as we hurt so painfully?

Our healing requires some form of restitution. Quite simply, what was taken from us must be replaced. While money cannot heal the psychological and physical destruction we have suffered and it cannot undo what has been done, it can help in the healing our pains and sufferings. Whites and others who receive privileges from the oppressor's system are morally obligated to assist us in acquiring a just compensation. As a matter of fact, when our ancestors were going through our holocaust, most of the world including the Americans, Europeans, Arabians, the Catholic Church, and Jewish Synagogues all profited directly from their pain and suffering.

We need to ask ourselves how some humans could subject other humans to such evilness as we have been subjected to. We have been taught and believe that an entity called Satan can. We also need to inquire as to why they yet do the same. Then we need to ask who was and who is involved in this evilness.

When we theologize about the judgment, we must discuss retribution. (Matt 16:27). The Bible claims you reap what you sow. God claims He is returning to judge the wicked. So the idea of retribution is thoroughly biblically grounded.

---

[151] Elijah Muhammad. *Message to the Black Man*. P.293

There is a race war going on in America and it is part of a larger struggle the world over. I could also say and be just as correct that it all connects to the cosmic struggle, the final struggle between the forces of evilness and righteousness.

Africans are growing impatient with the excuses and abuses of white people. Jesus also, became impatient with the moneychangers in the Temple, and utilized violence to drive them away.[152] How long will it be before Africans lose all their patience and hope and resort to violence? After all, Doctor Frantz Fanon, the African freedom fighter, has well taught us and would have many of us believe that perhaps,

> Violence alone, violence committed by the people, violence organized and educated by its leaders, makes it possible for the masses to understand social truths and gives the key to them. Without that struggle, without that knowledge of the practice of action, there's nothing but a fancy-dress parade and the blare of the trumpets. There's nothing save a minimum of re-adaptation, a few reforms at the top, a flag waving: and down there at the bottom an undivided mass, still living in the middle ages, endlessly marking time.[153]

The Tunisian, Jewish intellect and struggler against colonialism, Albert Memmi, was well aware that African Americans are going to wage the final violent struggle in the not too distant future. We either win or we lose. He goes by way of Malcolm X to make his point.

> For Malcolm X the final battle has begun; it is not, as Baldwin thinks, merely imminent; nor is it, as King sees it, a game of skill, endurance and

---

[152] *Matt* 21:12.
[153] Frantz Fanon, *The Wretched of the Earth* (N.Y. 1963) p.117.

> evasion tactics. It is a real conflict; a battle to the death; if is being fought with clubs and with dogs, and from time to time murder is committed, though the blacks for the moment are not in a position to retaliate. In the meantime they have to prepare for the showdown, and above all to raise the moral of their troops.[154]

The war is going on, and has been ongoing since the so-called Aryans swept down from the northernmost mountains and steppes of Europe and began their marching towards world domination. When will it end? Perhaps we (African Americans) will make a decision in the near future to "draw the line in the sand," or maybe it will last until Jesus makes His second entry into the world riding on a white cloud with a sword in his hand and accompanied by a legion of angels. We may not know the exact time or place of its end, but we do know it shall end. The bible informs us, "There is a time for everything, and a season for every activity under heaven."[155]

According to The Honorable Elijah Muhammad the final war can still be averted if America (white men) will halt her injustices against the black man.

> You don't need Navys, ground forces, air forces, standing armies to fight this last war. What America needs to win is to give freedom and equal justice to her slaves (the so-called Negroes). This injustice to her slaves is the real cause of this final war. Give them up to return to their own or divide with them the country that you took from their people (the Indians), which they have helped you to build up and maintain with, their sweat and blood for 400 years. They even gave all of their

---

[154] Albert Memmi, *Dominated Man* (Boston 1968) p.12.
[155] *Ecclesiastes*. 3:1-8. NIV, 1997

brain power to you. They helped you kill anyone that you said was your enemy; even if it was their own brother or your own brother. What have you given them for their labor and lives?[156]

The judgment must be made, but the outcome of this judgment will be determined by whether the white man acquires the right relationship with God. This implies that his relationship is right with his brother also. God's promise of his wrathful judgment is not unconditional. God hates what America is guilty of, but He has prepared a way she can travel and find her way back to Him. This way involves reconciliation with her brothers and sisters of this world and God.

> 21. I hate your show and pretence – your hypocrisy of honoring me with your religious assemblies. 22. I will not accept your burnt offerings and thank offerings. I will not look at your offerings of peace. 23. Away with your hymns and praise – they are mere noise to my ears. I will not listen to your music, no matter how lovely it is. 24. I want to see a mighty flood of justice-a torrent of doing good.[157]

White people need to get their act together while there is still time. They need to get it together while a forgiving God is still holding the flames of anger and vengeance at bay. They need to get it together and dispense justice and equality to those they have wronged for so many centuries. How can white people get it together? They can do so by doing everything they possibly can to heal the pain and suffering inflicted by their ancestors, their government, and many of the white citizenry on our ancestors and us today. They must repent of all that burdensome

---
[156] Elijah Muhammad. *Message to the Black Man*. Atlanta:1965 p. 298.
[157] *Amos* 5:21-24

sin. Will white America wake up and do what is right, or is it too late and the words of the prophet writer James Baldwin, "No more water, the fire next time," are already upon us all?

> The day of the Lord is surely coming, as unexpectedly as a thief, and then the heavens will pass away with a terrible noise and the heavenly bodies will disappear in fire, and the earth and everything on it will be burned up.[158]

THE END!!!

---

[158] *2 Peter* 3:10. The Living Bible. Holman Illus., Edit. N.Y.:1973.

Appendix

HUMAN RIGHTS

UNITED NATIONS CONVENTION ON THE PREVENTION AND PUNISHMENT OF GENOCIDE

Article I:
Genocide is a crime under international law whether committed in time of peace or in time of war.

Article II:
Genocide is "any of the following acts committed with intent to destroy, in whole or in part, a national, ethnical, racial or religious group such as:
(a) Killing members of the group.
(b) Causing serious bodily or mental harm to members of the group.
(c) Deliberately inflicting on the group conditions of life calculated to bring about its physical destruction in whole or in part.
(d) Imposing measures intended to prevent births within the group.
(e) Forcibly transferring children of the group to another group;

Article III:
Any of the following acts shall be punishable:
(a) Genocide
(b) Conspiracy to commit genocide;
(c) Direct and public incitement to commit genocide;
(d) Attempt to commit genocide;

(e) Complicity in genocide;
Article IV:
Persons committing genocide or any of the other acts enumerated in article III shall be punished, whether they are constitutionally responsible rulers, public officials or private individuals.

DECLARATION OF THE
RIGHTS OF MAN AND OF THE CITIZEN
Approved by the National Assembly of France, August 26, 1789.

The representatives of the French people, organized as a National Assembly, believing that the ignorance, neglect, or contempt of the rights of man are the sole cause of public calamities and of the corruption of governments, have determined to set forth in a solemn declaration the natural, unalienable, and sacred rights of man, in order that this declaration, being constantly before all the members of the Social body, shall remind them continually of their rights and duties; in order that the acts of the legislative power, as well as those of the executive power, may be compared at any moment with the objects and purposes of all political institutions and may thus be more respected, and, lastly, in order that the grievances of the citizens, based hereafter upon simple and incontestable principles, shall tend to the maintenance of the constitution and redound to the happiness of all. Therefore the National Assembly recognizes and proclaims, in the presence and under the auspices of the Supreme Being, the following rights of man and of the citizen:

Articles:
1.Men are born and remain free and equal in rights. Social distinctions may be founded only upon the general good.

2. The aim of all political association is the preservation of the natural and imprescriptibly rights of man. These rights are liberty, property, security, and resistance to oppression.

3. The principle of all sovereignty resides essentially in the nation. Nobody nor individual may exercise any authority which does not proceed directly from the nation.

4. Liberty consists in the freedom to do everything, which injures no one else; hence the exercise of the natural rights of each man has no limits except those, which assure to the other members of the society the enjoyment of the same rights. These limits can only be determined by law.

5. Law can only prohibit such actions as are hurtful to society. Nothing may be prevented which is not forbidden by law, and no one may be forced to do anything not provided for by law.

6. Law is the expression of the general will. Every citizen has a right to participate personally, or through his representative, in its foundation. It must be the same for all, whether it protects or punishes. All citizens, being equal in the eyes of the law, are equally eligible to all dignities and to all public positions and occupations, according to their abilities, and with-out distinction except that of their virtues and talents.

7. No person shall be accused, arrested, or imprisoned except in the cases and according to the forms prescribed by law. Any one soliciting, transmitting, executing, or causing to be executed, any arbitrary order shall be punished. But any citizen summoned or arrested in virtue of the law shall submit without delay, as resistance constitutes an offense.

8. The law shall provide for such punishments only as are strictly and obviously necessary, and no one shall suffer punishment except it be legally inflicted in virtue of a law passed and promulgated before the commission of the offense.

9. As all persons are held innocent until they shall have been declared guilty, if arrest shall be deemed indispensable, all harshness not essential to the securing of the prisoner's person shall be severely repressed by law.

10. No one shall be disquieted on account of his opinions, including his religious views, provided their manifestation does not disturb the public order established by law.

11. The free communication of ideas and opinions is one of the most precious of the rights of man. Every citizen may, accordingly, speak, write, and print with freedom, but shall be responsible for such abuses of this freedom as shall be defined by law.

12. The security of the rights of man and of the citizen requires public military forces. These forces are, therefore, established for the good of all and not for the personal advantage of those to whom they shall be intrusted.

13. A common contribution is essential for the maintenance of the public forces and for the cost of administration. This should be equitably distributed among all the citizens in proportion to their means.

14. All the citizens have a right to decide, either personally or by their representatives, as to the necessity of the public contribution; to grant this freely; to know to what uses it is put; and to fix the proportion, the mode of assessment and of collection and the duration of the taxes.

15. Society has the right to require of every public agent an account of his administration.

16. A society in which the observance of the law is not assured, nor the separation of powers defined, has no constitution at all.

17. Since property is an inviolable and sacred right, no one shall be deprived thereof except where public necessity, legally determined, shall clearly demand it, and then only on condition that the owner shall have been previously and equitably indemnified.

INTERNATIONAL LAW ON CRIMES AGAINST HUMANITY

International law recognizes that those who commit crimes against humanity must make reparations. The right to reparation is well recognized in international law. It has been defined by the Permanent Court of International Justice (the predecessor of the International Court of Justice) in these terms:

The essential principle contained in the actual notion of an illegal act - a principle which seems to be established by international practice and in particular by the decisions of arbitrage tribunals - is that reparation must, as far as possible, wipe out all the consequences of the illegal act and re-establish the situation which would, in all probability, have existed if that act had not been committed. Restitution in kind or, if this is not possible, payment of a sum corresponding to the value which a restitution in kind would bear; the award, if need be, of damages for loss sustained which would not be covered by restitution in kind or payment in place of it - such are the principles which should serve to determine the amount of compensation due for an act contrary to international law.[159]

REPARATIONS BILL FOR THE AFRICAN SLAVES IN THE UNITED STATES THE FIRST SESSION FORTIETH CONGRESS

March 11, 1867 Thaddeus Stevens of Pennsylvania H.R. 29
"Whereas it is due to justice, as an example to future times, that some future punishment should be inflicted on the people who constituted the "confederate States of America." both because they, declaring an unjust war against the United States for the purpose of destroying republican liberty and permanently establishing slavery, as well as, for the cruel and barbarous manner in which they conducted said war, in violation of all the laws of civilized warfare, and also to compel them to make some compensation for the damages and expenditures caused by the said war: Therefore, Be it enacted by the Senate and House of Representatives of the United States of America in

---

[159] Chorzow Factory Case, Germany vs. Poland (1928)

Congress assembled. That all the public lands belonging to the ten States that formed the government of the so-called confederate States of America shall be forfeited by said States and become forthwith vested in the United States.

"SEC. 2. And be it further enacted. That the President shall forthwith proceed to cause the seizure of such of the property belonging to the belligerent enemy as is deemed forfeited by the act of July 17, A. D. 1862, and hold and appropriate the same as enemy's property, and to proceed to condemnation with that already seized.

"SEC. 3. And be it further enacted, That in lieu of the proceeding to condemn the property thus seized enemy's property. as is provided by the act of July A. D. 1862, two commissions or more, as by him may be deemed necessary, shall be appointed by the President for each of the said "confederate States,"to consist of three persons each, one of whom shall be an officer of the late or present Army, and two shall be civilians, neither of whom shall be citizens of the State for which he shall be appointed; that the said commissions shall proceed adjudicate and Condemn the property foresaid, under such forms and proceedings is shall be prescribed by the Attorney General of the United States, whereupon the title to said property shall become vested in the United States.

"SEC. 4. And be it further enacted. That out of the lands thus seized and confiscated the slaves who have been liberated by the operations of the war and the amendment to the constitution or otherwise, who resided in said "confederate States" on the 4th day of March, A. D. 1861, or since, shall have distributed to them as follows, namely: to each male person who is the head of a family, forty acres; to each adult male, whether the head of a family or not, forty acres, to each widow who is the head of a family, forty acres-to be held by them in fee-simple, but to be inalienable for the next ten years after they become seized thereof. For the purpose of distributing and allotting said land the Secretary of War shall appoint as many commissions in each State as he shall deem necessary, to consist of three members each, two of whom at least shall not be citizens of the State for which he is appointed. Each of said commissioners shall receive a salary of $3,000 annually and all his necessary expenses. Each commission shall be allowed one clerk, whose salary shall be $2,000 per annum homestead aforesaid shall be vested in trustees for the use of the liberated persons aforesaid. Trustees shall be appointed by the Secretary of War, and shall receive such salary as he shall direct, not exceeding $3,000 per annum. At the end of ten years the, absolute title to said homesteads shall be conveyed to said owners or to the heirs of such as are then dead.

"SEC. 5. And be it further enacted, That out of the balance of the property thus seized and confiscated there shall be raised, in the manner hereinafter provided, a sum equal to fifty dollars, for each homestead, to be applied by the trustees hereinafter mentioned toward the erection of buildings on the said homesteads for the use of said slaves; and the further sum of $500,000,000, which shall be appropriated as follows, to wit: $200,000,000 shall be invested in United States six per cent, securities; and the interest thereof shall be semi-annually added to the pensions allowed by law to pensioners who have become so by reason of the late war; $300,000,000, or so much thereof as may be need, shall be appropriated to pay damages done to loyal citizens by the civil or military Operations of the government lately called the "confederate States of America."

Bibliography

And suggested further reading.

Aptheker, Herbert. *Negro Slave Revolts.* N.Y., 1939.
Baker, Lillian. *The Japanning of America.* Medford, 1991.
Bennett, Lerone Jr. *Confrontation: Black and White.* Baltimore, 1965.
--------*Black Power U.S.A.* Chicago, 1967.
Benton-Lewis, Dorothy. *Black Reparations.* Maryland, 1978.
Berry, Mary Frances. *Black Resistance, White Law.* N.Y., 1994.
Boller, P. & Story, R. *A More Perfect Union. Documents in U.S. History.* Vol, 1. Princeton, N.J., 1988.
Book Of Jasher. N.Y., 1840
Boutelle, Paul. *The Case for a Black Party.* N.Y., 1968
Browne, Robert. *Should the U.S. Be Partitioned.* N.Y., 1968.
Burning Spear. *Black People and the U.S. Economy.* Oakland, 1982.
Clarke, John Henrik. *Christopher Columbus and the African Holocaust.* Brooklyn, 1982.
Conot, Robert. *Rivers of Blood, Years of Darkness.* N.Y., 1967.
Degler, Carl N. *Out of Our Past.* N.Y., 1970.
D'orso, Michael. *Rosewood: Like Judgement Day.* N.Y., 1996.
DuBois, W.E.B. *Black Reconstruction.* N.Y., 1962.
Fanon, Frantz. *The Wretched of the Earth.* N.Y., 1963.
Genovese, Eugene D. *The Political Economy of Slavery.* N.Y., 1967.
Ginsburg, Ralph. *100 Years of Lynchings.* Baltimore, 1988.
Grant, Joanne. *Black Protest: Historical Documents and Analyses.* N.Y., 1968.
Grier, William H. and Price Cobbs. *Black Rage.* N.Y., 1992.
Grimshaw, Allen D. *Racial Violence in the United States.* Chicago, 1969.
Hacker, Andrew. *Two Nations: Black and White, Separate, Hostile, Unequal.* N.Y. 1995.
Holy Bible. *King James*, edition
.... *New American* Standard, edition
Hayden, Tom. *Rebellion in Newark.* N.Y., 1967.
Hersey, John. *The Algiers Incident.* N.Y., 1968.
Hood, Robert E. *Begrimed And Black.* Minneapolis: 1994.
Huggins, Nathan. *Black Odyssey.* N.Y., 1977.

James, C.L.R. *The Black Jacobins.* N.Y., 1962.
Lecky, Robert S. and H. Elliott Wright. *Black Manifesto.* N.Y., 1969.
Madow, Leo. Anger: How to Recognize and Cope With It. N.Y., 1972.
Mannix, Daniel P. and Malcolm Cowley. *Black Cargoes.* N.Y., 1962.
Memmi, Albert. *The Colonized and the Colonizer.* N.Y., 1965.
-------*Dominated Man.* Boston, 1968.
Munford, Clarence J. *Race and Reparations.* Trenton, 1996.
Myrdal, Gunnar. *An American Dilemma.* N.Y., 1072.
Obadele, Imari Abubakari. *War in America.* Detroit, 1968.
-------*The Republic of New Africa.* New Orleans, 1970's.
-------*Reparations Yes!* 4th edition. Baton Rouge. 1995.
Patterson, William L. *We Charge Genocide.* N.Y., 1970.
Pettigrew, Thomas F. *A Profile of the Negro American.* New Jersey, 1964.
Pope-Hennessy, John. *A Study of the Atlantic Slave Trade.* N.Y., 1967.
Pross, Christian. *Paying for the Past.* Baltimore, 1998.
Schedler, George. *Racist Symbols & Reparations.* N.Y., 1998.
Schuker, Stephen A. *American Reparations to Germany, 1919-33: Implications for the Third-World Debt Crisis.* Princeton, 1988.
Segal, Ronald. The *Race War.* N.Y., 1966.
Shabazz, Amilcar. *The Forty Acres Documents.* Baton Rouge, 1994.
Stamp, Kenneth M. *The Peculiar Institution.* N.Y., 1956.
Tannenbaum, Frank. *Slave & Citizen.* N.Y., 1946.
Tattersfield, Nigel. *The Forgotten Trade.* London, 1991.
Turner, William. *The Police Establishment.* N.Y., 1968.
White, Anne Terry. *Human Cargo.* Champaign, 1972.
White, John and Ralph Willett. *Slavery in the American South.* N.Y.,1970.
Williams, Eric. *Capitalism & Slavery.* N.Y., 1966.

www.ingramcontent.com/pod-product-compliance
Lightning Source LLC
Chambersburg PA
CBHW051103160426
43193CB00010B/1302